Table of Contents

The Phone Call 2

Sign, Sign Everywhere a Sign........................ 7

When You Lose, Don't Lose the Lesson 12

Shut-Up! Shut-Up!...................................... 16

Know Your Role...................................... 19

Playing Politics.. 23

Fireworks Can Be Loud 25

Transition Year of 2007 30

The Consolidation and the Home Rule Charter......... 36

Running for Mayor.................................... 45

Starting Down the Path of Change 53

The Three Puzzle Pieces.............................. 62

A Very Interesting First Year..................................... 69

Josh Morris 75

Jim Huntsinger 81

How a Municipal Government Operates.................. 92

Red Tape, Process and Zoning 107

Everyone is Paid to Think 116

Tornados... 124

Expectations from the Top 130

Overcoming Turnover in the Same Department..... 136

Some Lessons are Verbal
Some Lessons are Written 141

Restraint of Power is the
Ultimate Exercise of Power 143

Tragedy 146

Betty Called, We Listened.. 150

Appointments, Lots of Them..................................... 155

Chain the Doors Call the Press 159

School District Change and the S.A.C. 163

Leadership is not for those
that want to be in charge.. 167

Short Stories from the
Front Line of a Municipality.................................... 169

The Phone Call

Being mayor is the ultimate backstage pass to small town government. Drama, humor, and pathos are inevitable as the mayor works with the best and the worst building a strong community. In Republic, Missouri, population around 17,000, the mayor can be involved in anything. Most days, we successfully solved community problems. Some days I thought humanity had lost its way. Occasionally, I had to figure out who pays for lunch. The mayor position is one of leadership, compassion and decision making. Less minutiae, more vision. Let's take a tour. I will introduce you to the characters. We can use my backstage pass.

My municipal involvement started with a phone call in late 2004. A Republic, Missouri city council member, Tony Stephens had resigned. Mayor Jim Collins was looking for a replacement for him in Ward 3. Republic is a community in Greene County located in southwest Missouri just to the west of Springfield. The population is around 17,000 and has grown for the last several censuses. The city was divided into 4 wards with 2 representatives in each ward. The terms were two years and each ward had a council member up for election every year. The mayor position was also a two-year term elected at-large from the entire city. The phone call was from a council member at the time in ward 3, Carol Lohkamp. She thought of me when it came time to fill the position. She suggested that I call the mayor and see if he would appoint me to the council. I called Mayor Collins to inquire about the open position.

Mayor Jim Collins was a bi-vocational pastor. He worked at a variety of jobs, from selling newspapers to giving roofing estimates and preaching every Sunday at a small Baptist Church. At the time, Mayor Collins was in his mid-50's and already had a heart attack. I called Mayor Collins (we had never met) and told him that Carol had called me about the position. He stated that he had already filled the position with a man named Brian Vanderschaaf. The mayor was never one to turn down a volunteer and asked me to serve on the Brookline consolidation committee. Mayor Collins later told me that Mr. Vanderschaaf was chosen since he had worked on Mayor Collins election campaign at the previous election.

The Brookline consolidation committee was a group of appointed individuals to walk through the upcoming consolidation of the village of Brookline and the city of Republic. Brookline was a small community of around 400 citizens with a storied history. The Young brothers had a shoot-out with the local sheriff and killed 5 law enforcement officers in January 1932. It was known as the Young Brothers Massacre and prompted a nationwide manhunt for the brothers. One interesting fact is that the Young brother's first kill was the marshal of nearby Republic in 1929.

In the early 2000's, Brookline was still a very small community of about 400 people. It had a very large footprint in the area northeast of Republic and west of Springfield, Missouri. The Brookline government had a board of alderman, a treasurer and a board president/mayor. Brookline did not have any services that it owned, leased or any type of emergency services. Almost all homes and businesses were on well water and had septic tanks. Emergency services were provided by the Greene County Missouri sheriff's department along with mutual aid from the city of

Republic and Springfield. Fire protection was through a local fire district where each household inside the district would pay an annual real estate tax for their fire protection. It was an all-volunteer department.

The Brookline leadership started talks with the city of Republic leadership about a consolidation of the two communities. The mayors of both communities appointed individuals from each area and formed the Brookline consolidation committee. As a committee, we discussed a variety of issues that would need to be addressed if the consolidation passed a vote by the two communities. We also addressed issues at the time and potential solutions for those issues with those recommendations being sent to the mayor's and the city administrator of Republic at the time, Dean Thompson. If the citizens voted for consolidation, one new ward with two new council members would be added from Brookline to the City of Republic for a period of two years. After the two years, that additional ward would be rolled into one of the other wards and the council would return to four wards.

Once I was on the committee, Mayor Collins told me that he was glad that he got to know me and told me he would like to see me run for a council seat in Ward 3. An appointed council member was only on council until the next election; therefore, they did not fill the remaining term of the council member that left, regardless of the time remaining on that term. A quick side note, if an appointed council member decided to run at the next election from their appointment and it was the same time as the other council member in that same ward then both were up for election. The one receiving the most votes would receive the two-year term and the one receiving the second number of votes would receive a one-year term.

Being involved in public service had not really crossed my mind at that point in my life. Public service in a community in which I was a relative outsider was not on the top of my involvement list, especially in Republic with its political past. We were involved with our church, had kids to raise and all the fun that being an adult can give. My family past had plenty of community involvement and that may have influenced my quick decision when Carol called me that day. Growing up in Coffeyville, Kansas, our family was involved at our church where my father was a deacon and my mother worked with various groups inside and outside the church. My father was also on the Coffeyville Community College Board of Trustees for several years along with being Chairman of the Board of Trustees for a few additional years. My mother was the Finance Director and Assistant City Manager for the City of Coffeyville, Kansas. After she retired, she worked for the Red Cross as their finance director for a few more years until she fully retired from professional life. While in high school and throughout my four years in college, I worked at an electric company in Coffeyville, Liebert Brothers Electric. The company was owned by three gentlemen, Al Liebert, Bob Liebert and Emil Roesky. Al Liebert was the mayor of Coffeyville for several years when I worked there. So, I was surrounded by community service growing up, but did not really have the drive or calling to be involved until the day Carol called. My motivation to return Carol's call seemed to be the fact that I wanted to bring a sensible approach to governing along with a business background to help move the community forward. After witnessing what my parents dealt with regarding their community service, it was my thought my business world experience could be beneficial to the community. There was not any particular topic or subject that I felt needed addressed or solved. Many people have one or two issues that they want to change and run for public office on those agendas. They believe if the issue is affecting them, it is affecting others and they will have some resonance with the community on the issue causing the citizens to vote for them. That seems to be how politicians want to connect with the community. In my case, I had very little interaction with the city government of Republic like the majority of citizens; therefore, there was not anything that motivated me to be involved other than I thought my background, experience and sensible thought process could benefit the community in which we lived.

Sign, Sign Everywhere a Sign

The first election for me was in April, 2005, I was 36 at the time. Sign-up consisted of five consecutive weeks starting in the first week of December. At that time, the person that signed up first had their name on the ballot first. My timing was off, as I was out of town on the first sign-up day. The incumbent was Brian Vanderschaaf. He was the first to sign up on that first day. Mayor Collins found out that I was second on the ballot and he told me that being an unknown in the community, second on the ballot and going against an incumbent was one of the most difficult things to overcome in politics. His advice was to get out and knock on the doors of my ward along with introducing myself to a few local entities, like the Kiwanis club, Chamber of Commerce and other council members.

My campaign did not consist of much. We had 65 cardboard signs created and fliers. The signs were white with red lettering. The signs were simple, easily read at 30 mph and emphasized the last name. In Missouri, if a candidate for public office spent over a certain amount, they had to file a form in the state office along with all their financials and their campaign contributors. We did not spend much on the signs since they did not come with any type of mounting stake and stayed under the state threshold for submitting campaign financials. Most signs now are corrugated plastic and come with a two-wire post for the ground. Mine were not that fancy. My signs were one sided, on cardboard and needed to be stapled to a stake for the ground. Since every person running for public office had a campaign manager, I figured I would get a campaign manager that could really help me. I called the person that built our home in Republic, David Pittman. He jumped at the chance and said he would help in any way. What we needed at that point were stakes for the signs. David arrived the next day with about 80 wooden stakes he had cut from scrap lumber at one of his construction sites.

We strategically placed the signs in yards of people we talked with, focusing on high traffic areas along the main streets within the ward. We also asked our subdivision owner permission for a special sign on Election Day. The signs were stapled to the stake after it was driven in the ground with a sledgehammer. Yes, a sledgehammer. It was southwest Missouri, after all, with rocks everywhere. Remarkably, the signs held up to rain, wind and the occasional lawnmower that would knock one down.

The fliers were on a 4"x10" piece of green paper. It was all black ink and had my picture on it that my wife Diane took of me while I was lounging on the couch one day. It was not a planned picture for the flier; it was more of a casual picture that she would put in a scrapbook. My goal was to put a flier on the door or hand the flier to the person that answered the door as we made the rounds the weekend before the election. Those plans did not actually come to fruition.

Several months before the election, I had gone to the doctor about some breathing issues. He had a variety of questions about my breathing and checked my lungs for capacity as part of the regular review. He stated that my lungs sounded normal and asked me why I thought I have issues. My story caught his attention, albeit that it was a simple story. I was sitting at the counter one evening eating a bowl of cereal. Cereal was not one of my favorites to eat and did not fully realize the reason for my distaste of the stuff. My wife came in the room and asked me why I was breathing so hard through my mouth while trying to eat the cereal. It was at that moment I realized I could barely breathe through my nose. Try pinching your nose and eating a spoonful of cereal. That is exactly what it was like for me. The doctor checked my nose and noticed that there was some severe blockage in both sides. He sent me to see an Ear, Nose and Throat doctor, Dr. Allan Allphin.

Dr. Allphin immediately knew the issues upon looking in my nostrils. One side contained a deviated septum causing blockage. On the other side a bone spur had caused blockage. In both sides, the turbinates were overly large and swollen causing increased blockage. Turbinates are small sac like structures in the nose that humidify and cleanse the incoming air. There are three sizes of turbinates in each nostril. According to Dr. Allphin, each side was 90% blocked thus causing breathing issues. Dr. Allphin recommended surgery to correct all the issues at once. The only issue was scheduling the surgery. The only date available was the Thursday before the election. The surgery would have me chair bound for several days since I would not be able to lie down to sleep and the surgery maintenance would have me up several times during the night. The splints in my nose required quite a bit of maintenance.

With the election the Tuesday after my surgery, the weekend after my surgery was the only time to pass out the fliers. With over 500 fliers on green paper, my wife came to the rescue. She and our daughter Nichole contacted our neighbors, the Ormsby's for assistance. Diane asked Cheryl Ormsby if she and her daughter would help pass out the fliers in the ward. Cheryl agreed along with their daughter, so Diane, Cheryl and the two daughters went canvassing ward 3 handing out fliers. My instructions were simple, knock on the door, tell them that I am running for the ward 3 council position, ask them to please vote and then leave. They were instructed not to ask for the vote, just ask them to be sure to get out and vote.

The Saturday before the election, Diane and her entourage passed out almost all the fliers in ward 3. Ironically, Brian Vanderschaaf was also walking the streets handing out fliers and talking with the citizens. Mr. Vanderschaaf actually came by our house not knowing it was our house. My son answered the door and Vanderschaaf recognized him. I was in a reclining chair in the front room and could see the door. I invited Vanderschaaf into the house, he sat down and we talked for about 30 minutes on a variety of topics. He left and ran into Diane at several houses in our neighborhood.

Election Day was interesting. My nose splints were still in place and we had one more sign to install. My special sign was a series of signs that would be put on our subdivision property across from the election booths at the community center. The community center was a recreational facility for the city of Republic. It contained two indoor basketball courts, meeting rooms, indoor walking track, exercise facility and a variety of other areas for events. As with all elections in the states of Missouri, there is a law against electioneering within 25 feet of the front door to the voting site. This usually meant that there would be a plethora of signs right at that the 25-foot mark and at every location leading up to the doors. Not wanting to get lost in the mix of signs, we strategically placed many of our signs at the corners to the parking lot where no one else was putting signs.

The special sign was a "Burma-shave" type sign on the subdivision property. A Burma-shave sign was a series of roadside signs with very few words on each sign. The signs would be spread apart along the road and would be read as the traveler moved down the road. The entire advertising message would be known at the end of the last sign. The majority of people voting at that location would be travelling from the east going west. Our large sign was on south, not the best location, but north side was city property and we could not use that side. The first sign said "Vote", the second sign had "For", and the third sign had "BUCKNER" with the fourth sign stating "WARD 3". The sign caught everyone's attention and seemed to be more effective than the other types of signs.

Mayor Collins was not correct in his assessment, second on the ballot, unknown and against an incumbent. The vote count went 177-113 in my favor. My thought is that the fliers being handed out by the ladies and the Burma-shave sign won the election. I did not knock on one door or go to any civic organizations. That election win started twelve years of municipal service with many highlights.

When You Lose,
Don't Lose the Lesson

Municipal government is interesting at all levels, regardless of size. Any organization, government or business, can get off track or lose its way during meetings. In public government meetings, Robert's Rules of Order give an outline for conducting public meetings. At the city of Republic, we followed Robert's Rules and attempted to ensure that we did not enter any discussion that was not on the agenda or that violated the Sunshine Law of transparency. The Sunshine Law defined public access to government records that included rules for meeting postings. There are different tactics inside a meeting that can go on in which the average citizen would not know to use, me included. One evening in 2005, we were discussing what to do with an old fire truck that was in disrepair and out of service for our department. It was one of the first trucks ever purchased by the city. According to Chief Duane Compton, the truck was originally purchased by the city in 1962 and took possession in 1963. The new 1962 American LaFrance fire truck was originally going to be driven back to Republic by Republic citizen Bob Duvall and another citizen, but the dealer shipped it to the city of Republic by rail car. The railroad went directly through the middle of town, so access to the delivery was easy, but offloading the truck was an issue. The solution encompassed unhooking the rail cars and moving the rail car with the truck to a side track. The side track ended at an old rail depot that had a large concrete loading dock that was the same height as the rail car. The fire department drove the truck off the rail car, onto the concrete loading dock and on the street. At the council meeting, the local Kiwanis club showed an interest in keeping the vehicle to restore it and use it in parades. The fire chief, Duane Compton, had a restoration shop in St. Louis that was willing to take the fire truck, restore it and keep it in their museum with the city of Republic logo on the doors as it would have been when new. After working on and restoring a car myself, I knew the Kiwanis would have a hard time raising the funds and finding someone to restore the vehicle, let alone getting it running and passing an inspection to participate in a parade.

The council discussion was a spirited one with me taking the side of sending it to St. Louis and the other seven council members taking the side of the Kiwanis. The chief was on my side, but could not publicly state that opinion, as he was to remain neutral being a staff member. He could give a recommendation, but at that time, the department leaders were instructed not to push their recommendations. Josh Morris from ward 1 seemed to take the lead from the outset of the conversation and we had some excellent discussion, even though we were on opposite sides. Just when I thought my argument was getting through to some of the council members, the other representative from ward 1, Don Murray, called for the question. His motion was seconded and that was that for the discussion. I did not know what happened, since there was not a municipal training guide or glossary of terms for a new council member. A call for the question is a procedural move to end the discussion and vote. It is a tactic to use if a council member thought the discussion was fully covered or going on too long. The vote went 1-7 in defeat, lesson learned. Ironically, Don Murray was the first full-time paid fire chief for the city of Republic. After the meeting, I made the comment to several of the council members and the fire chief that the city would end up with that fire truck in the future and it would be in worse shape than it was at that time.

Knowing the process of how a government or a business operates is a key to being successful. Who are the "go-to" people in most organizations? They are usually the people that are experts in their field or the ones that completely understand the process of the organization. When you do not know the "go-to" person in the organization, it will be up you to learn the process on your own or ask those that have been there or have vast experience. There are times when the lingo of an organization is just as important as the process for clear communication. Not every organization will train on the process or lingo, therefore to become a more valuable team member delve into the process and lingo on your own. It will take some time and possibly repetition to completely understand the process or lingo but once that knowledge is fully understood, you become more of an asset to the organization. Some of the learning could be trial by fire or on the job experience. In my case, not fully knowing the nuances of how the council operated caused the vote to go the other way. It was part of the governing process and in this case, I lost the vote. When you lose, do not lose the lesson.

Side story: It was 2012 and I was in my third term as Mayor. The city administrator, Jim Krischke, had a meeting with Chief Duane Compton. When Jim and chief called from Jim's office and had me on speaker phone, the first words from the chief were, "You were right when you said we would own the old fire truck again." The Kiwanis had contacted him and wanted to know if the city "wanted" the fire truck back. We

discussed it and decided to put it before council....
again. This time the recommendation was to send the
truck to the restoration shop in St. Louis and go with
the original plan.   Chief Compton contacted the
gentleman at the restoration shop and he was willing
to take possession of the truck. The vote was 8-0 to
send the truck to St. Louis. Hindsight may be 20/20,
but foresight can be 20/20 also.

Shut-Up! Shut-Up!

City councils, county boards and municipal elected bodies are made up of citizens with little or no experience in government or public meetings. Robert's Rules and the Sunshine Law should be followed and executed for the best meeting results. When one of these is broken, meetings can get out of hand quickly. In May 2006, Mayor Collins enforced a Sunshine Law rule to the degree that may have cost him a future election. During that discussion in May 2006, a council member from ward 4, O.K. Armstrong, entered into a discussion on a topic that was not part of the agenda topic. The agenda topic encompassed a rezoning of a 129-acre plat that went from one zoning classification to another. Mr. Armstrong attempted to discuss the city's transportation plan and how it needed to be changed. This was not an item on the agenda as required by the Sunshine Law. Discussing the city's transportation plan as it pertained to the plat we were discussing would have been acceptable and probably part of the discussion. In this case Mr. Armstrong attempted to enter a discussion on the transportation plan overall contents and where things needed to be changed around the city. When Mr. Armstrong attempted to go down that path, Mayor Collins interrupted him and said that it was not part of the discussion of the rezone. Mr. Armstrong attempted to discuss it again and this time the mayor interrupted him immediately. Someone in the audience took up for Mr. Armstrong and stated that they thought Mr. Armstrong had the floor. Mayor Collins apparently felt the need to address the audience member and stated there would not be any comments from the audience. At this point, Mr. Armstrong attempted to discuss the overall transportation plan again, when the mayor abruptly said, "Shut-up, shut-up" and then instructed the police chief to remove Mr. Armstrong. Mr. Armstrong was escorted out the door by police Chief Mark Lowe.

The front page of the local paper at the time, The Republic Monitor, had the headline of "Shut-up, shut-up". Although the circulation of the paper was not large, it was the lead headline above the fold and everywhere papers were being sold, it was the only thing anyone saw. In 2007, Mayor Collins decided to not run for mayor at the next election time in April 2008, but to run for a state legislative position in the 134th District at that time, which included the city of Republic. That position was held by Jim Viebrock who was an incumbent on his second term and a Republic hometown guy. Part of the campaign against Mayor Collins was the issue from 2006 with the council member that was removed from the meeting. Subsequently, Mayor Collins lost the race for the State office. Jim Viebrock won again. Following the Sunshine Law is necessary for any public meeting. The handling of this situation by Mayor Collins may have cost him the election. Enforce the Sunshine Law, follow Robert's Rules of Order and handle any deviation with professionalism and courtesy. Lesson learned.

Many municipal governments and many organizations get off course when the process or in this case the rules are not followed. There are two facets of this issue. The first facet is the council member that did not follow the Sunshine Law. There are rules and then there are laws. Each has its own repercussions. The city could be fined for not following the Sunshine

Law. The council member did not make that a priority when he chose to go down a path that potentially violated the Sunshine Law. The second facet is how the mayor handled the situation. The mayor was notably frustrated at the council member due to his lack of compliance to the mayor's request of keeping within the realm of the Sunshine Law and the conversation at hand. It would have been more prudent to adjourn the meeting for fifteen to twenty minutes and hold a private conversation with the council member, the mayor and the city attorney outlining the Sunshine Law. It would have given everyone time to relax and review the conversation in their minds before proceeding.

In leadership, situations will come your way that you did not create or cause, but it will require you to act. How you respond could define your leadership for the future. People remember words and actions. In this case the mayor's words and action were immortalized in the newspaper. Never let your emotions override your cognitive ability to make a logical decision.

Know Your Role

U pon my arrival on city council, Mayor Collins met with me and explained my role in the process of elected government. He outlined that our role as council members included reviewing the bills that are presented to us from staff, ask any pertinent questions and vote up or down on the bill. The mayor also stated that he would never tell us how to vote, which would get tested quickly. The overview provided me with some framework on what to expect. It did not provide me with the exact process of a council meeting or the lingo that accompanied the process. Each council member had been told the same thing, however some elected officials in communities attempt to go beyond their role and try to influence things that they feel need their attention. This is where most councils or groups head off course.

We had an opening on city council. Mayor Collins had plans to appoint another pastor to the council. He was a pastor at another Baptist church in town and the mayor thought he would be a good addition to the council. It did not make a difference to me whether he was a pastor or a Baptist or anything else. What mattered was whether he would be able to govern without prejudice, understand his role and be able to effectively communicate his thoughts and ideas. In his monologue the meeting before we were to vote on his candidate, the mayor in an open meeting stated that, "When you vote to approve him, we will have a full council again." Most council members did not catch the phrasing. The next meeting would be the vote and I met with the mayor before the meeting. I told him that in his conversation with me about the role of council members, he stated that he would never tell us how to vote. I told him that he had done that very thing the week before with his comment. He acknowledged that he had made that comment and apologized. In municipal government, the slightest misstep in phrasing can be taken a variety of ways by anyone that hears it. In this case, all our council meetings were televised on the local cable channel and anyone that watched the meeting would have heard it as well.

When it came time to vote for the appointee, I took my time and looked at Mayor Collins, looked at the appointee and then back to Mayor Collins. I voted to appoint him and that started many years of service for that appointee, however I wanted to ensure Mayor Collins knew that my vote could have easily gone the other way because of how he handled us as a council. He knew it and I knew and that is all that mattered at that point. Silence can be used as effective communication.

Mayor Collins held a luncheon every month with all the council members present along with the department leaders. The luncheon was designed to discuss topics that were not on the agenda in an open forum. The citizens were invited to attend, along with anyone else. The city clerk, who had just been hired, brought up the issue that these meetings were de facto council meetings. According to the Missouri Sunshine Law at the time, more than three members together would constitute a potential meeting and needed to be posted correctly. An unposted meeting was in conflict with the Sunshine Law. With all the council members in attendance and without a set agenda or a posted meeting notice, the luncheons were potentially a Sunshine Law violation. Mayor Collins put together an agenda for the meetings and began posting the meeting agenda within the allotted number of hours before the luncheon. The agendas turned out to be the upcoming council meeting agendas and most of the discussion took place at the luncheons and not at the council meetings. This did not seem to sit well with most of the citizens that attended the regular meetings and it did not set well with one citizen, one Betty North. Betty has an entire section for her involvement later. The luncheons continued throughout Mayor Collins tenure, though.

After I became mayor, the luncheons were ended and a new policy established with the city administrator. To alleviate any topics that might be discussed at a meeting where the topics were not on the agenda, each council member had an hour of the city administrators time each month to discuss anything they wanted. This was for the council members benefit, as well as, a benefit to the staff and city. The one-hour meetings helped the council members have their topics discussed and protected against any type of Sunshine Law violation. It helped the staff that the council members were not attempting to give direction where it was not needed.

I met each new council member reviewing their role and adding several important items to the conversation. Their role was to represent their ward and the individuals across the city in any decisions that council will have to make. Council members were there to ask pertinent questions, vote on the items before them and participate in moving the city forward. Additionally, their role was not to call department leaders and instruct them to do something or to contact any staff member with any type of direction or work project. All communication from council members would go through the city administrator, all communication. Establishing communication guidelines, boundaries of structure and establishing work processes are essential in keeping an organization moving forward efficiently.

The council members knew their roles, knew the Sunshine Law and had the opportunity to meet with the city administrator once a month to voice their concerns on any subject. Interestingly, usually five or six out of the eight council members would meet with the city administrator on a regular basis. The council could change members every election period, but the number meeting with the city administrator would not change often. During my eight years as mayor, there was not one month where all the council members met with the city administrator. It was not by design. It was that we always had council members that did not choose to meet.

While a council member, I would inquire how certain decisions were made within the city. The city administrator at the time and Mayor Collins were always very willing to let me know the decision-making process. Coming from a business background, it was at times difficult to see how many steps were involved in making a decision at a government level. There were times that I would offer my opinions and advice on how to work through to the decision quicker. Mayor Collins always listened to my points and would ask questions when he did not understand something. One phrase that I quickly picked up was his phrase, "I will take it under advisement." This let me know the conversation was over and he had what he needed from our conversation. He implemented a few of my suggestions and took the rest under advisement. That was excellent lesson for me to learn as a leader. Conclude a conversation when enough has been heard and end it with class.

Playing Politics

E very community and organization contains some sort of politics within itself. We often associate politics in government only settings, as if they hold the monopoly on political actions. What most people do not realize is that school districts, churches, businesses, non-profits and every other organization within a community operate with politics. Try getting on a school board against a long serving incumbent or attempt to instill a directional change to a local nonprofit. One will find out very quickly how political organizations are within a community. For years, Republic was known as a political community around southwest Missouri. It did change slightly under Mayor Collins. It became calmer from the previous years. A long serving member of the council, Jim Huntsinger was a representative from ward 4. He had served as the mayor pro-tem for Mayor Collins since the mayor's first mayoral election win in 2004. In 2006, Jim lost an election and the council had to elect a new mayor pro tem. The council elected me as the mayor pro tem. In 2007, Mr. Huntsinger ran again, this time unopposed. He was elected. He was lobbying for the mayor pro tem position again among the other council members. Every year at the first meeting after the election, the council would elect a mayor pro tem. The mayor would open the floor for nominations, then would wait for a second before asking for further nominations. Once all the nominations were heard, the mayor would call for a vote on each candidate. In most cases, one nomination was usually given and the council would not nominate further. Knowing this, Mr.

Huntsinger called a few council members asking them to nominate him. Mr. Huntsinger was a member of the mayor's church congregation. Many of the council members thought it would be better to have someone other than a member of the mayor's church as the mayor pro tem. One council member that was lobbied was council member Garry Wilson. Mr. Wilson was retired from a Kraft cheese processing plant. Mr. Wilson had been on council almost as long as Mr. Huntsinger. Mr. Wilson called me and stated that he had been lobbied by Mr. Huntsinger and the mayor to nominate Mr. Huntsinger as the mayor pro tem. Mr. Wilson made it very clear to me that he was going to nominate someone, but it would not be Mr. Huntsinger. It would be me. He did not tell that to the mayor or Mr. Huntsinger though.

The meeting that night did not go as the mayor or Mr. Huntsinger had planned. When the mayor opened the floor for nominations, Mr. Wilson raised his hand first. The mayor called on him immediately. The mayor knew from Mr. Huntsinger that Mr. Wilson would be nominating someone, fully expecting it was going to be Mr. Huntsinger. Mr. Wilson then nominated me. Mr. Huntsinger could see what was going to happen and graciously asked that the nominations be closed. A second was given and the nominations ceased. The vote was 7-0-1, with me abstaining from voting for myself. Mr. Huntsinger would go on to be the mayor pro tem for several years during my mayor tenure. He never again used politics inside the city, was an outstanding member of council and an excellent mayor pro tem.

Fireworks Can Be Loud

As a council member many items were brought before us that were intended as either information for the council or asking council members to decide on their particular item. While on council, we were given a presentation by a citizen that also worked for Greene County. This person wanted the council to consider banning the sale and use of fireworks in the city limits of Republic. Republic was one of the few communities that still allowed fireworks to be purchased and used on the 4th of July. Springfield to the east of Republic did not allow fireworks to be purchased or used within their city limits. It worked out for Republic, since we did have a few purchases from Springfield citizens. Personally, our subdivision put on a very large fireworks display on the 4th of July. Our subdivision display started with our family putting on our display for our family and a few friends. My enjoyment of fireworks was inherited from my father. My father was the youngest of four children and was born during the depression in 1932. His father (my grandfather) passed away in 1934. As a single mother, my grandmother raised four kids on a teacher's salary. The oldest child was 12 years older than my father; therefore, Christmas time was tough and my grandmother did her best to ensure everyone had something for Christmas. When my father was old enough, my grandmother would get him fresh fruit at Christmas along with a fireworks catalog. My grandmother could not afford too much, so by delaying my father's Christmas present a few months, she could do a little more for the older children. Therefore, my father would get his fruit and the fireworks catalog. He would spend days looking at the catalog and then submitting the order to his mother. She would order for a delivery in June and then pay for it when it arrived. My father would spend the days leading up to the 4th of July preparing the fuses to all the fireworks. On the 4th of July, he would then put on a fireworks display for the entire family. This tradition continued as we were growing up. We always had fireworks and always had a family fireworks display. When I was 12, my father took my brother (14 years old) and me fireworks shopping. My mother told us not to spend too much money, but with my father handling the fireworks financing, her advice was directed at him and not my brother or me. Upon arrival at the fireworks stand, my father handed my brother a twenty dollar bill and then handed me a twenty dollar bill. This was the old-style fireworks stand that was basically a little building with the fireworks on the back-counter display and you looked from the outside to see them. They do not make them like that anymore, since most are held in big tents. My brother and I would be allowed to purchase anything with my father guiding our purchases. Not sure how much he spent on top of our money, but he enjoyed it just as much as we did. After my brother and I were older, my father taught us how to make bottle rocket guns out of half inch conduit. It was not the best decision that we ever made, but it was another opportunity for my father to teach us how to be responsible with fireworks since the guns were used to shoot the bottle rockets into our pond at targets he put there for our use.

At the council meeting about the fireworks, the gentlemen giving the presentation went through every negative aspect of fireworks, which was expected since his goal was to have fireworks banned in the city in which he lived. He used his position at Greene County to get on the agenda with the city administrator at the time. Part of his sales pitch included letting us know how many other communities he had been to around southwest Missouri telling them the same thing and how they decided to ban fireworks after his presentation. At one point, council member Garry Wilson, the calmest and quietest of the council members, asked the gentlemen a question. After a minute or two of giving all the facts, Mr. Wilson asked the question again, since the gentlemen did not answer it. The gentlemen started on another sales pitch and that is when Mr. Wilson waved his right hand and said "Whoa. You need to answer my question." The only issue with Mr. Wilson waving his hand like he did was the fact that he sat to my left and I was leaning on the left facing the speaker to my right. His waved hand almost hit me directly in the face. Mr. Wilson was right about the gentleman not answering his question and wanted him to know that he had reached his limit with his dancing around the question. This is the first and only time I ever saw Mr. Wilson use his hands in a gesture and get visibly upset at a person speaking to the council. Mr. Wilson is the most reserved and calm person I ever met and it was a pleasure to serve with him for 12 years. After the gentlemen answered his question, he proceeded to tell us again that other communities were banning fireworks and those communities asked him to come there to present his point of view on the subject. I immediately asked him, "Who asked you to come here and present to this council?" He did not have an answer and immediately looked directly at Dean the city administrator. Nothing was said by either of them and there was an awkward silence for several seconds, so I repeated the question. After some additional delay, he stumbled around a little bit and stated that he thought Republic would want to hear the information like the other communities and follow what the other communities were doing. Good save. It was clear to me, all the other council members, the audience and everyone watching the meeting that he was there at the request of someone but he did not divulge that person. It was not a situation where he was looking out for the best interests of the community; he was looking out for his interests as well as the personal interests of the city administrator. My comments in return addressed the negative aspects that he mentioned in his comments.

It is always good to do your homework before a council meeting or any meeting. In this situation, the item was on the agenda at the beginning, so I knew it would be discussed and I accurately figured he would use statistics to prove his point. A few days before the meeting, I decided to do some research on traffic fatalities. I knew the July 4th time frame is one of the most traveled holidays during the year and wanted to know how much traffic fatalities increased during the 4th of July time frame. After reviewing some traffic data from the government and a few studies, I found out that July 2nd was one of the worst days for traffic fatalities in the United States. One study had it at number one in traffic fatalities. Interesting I thought. Not sure how it applies to the fireworks issue but decided to continue looking at facts. The data also indicated that July 3rd and July 5th were also in the top 6 or 7 days for traffic fatalities. So, here we have three of the worst days for traffic issues during the year around the same holiday. Armed with this information, I decided to apply it to his arguments. The gentlemen used statistics as part of his job regardless of what he was discussing; therefore, I would utilize statistics as well.

He stated he was there in front of our council of his own free will, which all of us knew was not true. I asked him if he knew the worst day for traffic fatalities in the U.S. during the year. He did not, so I explained to him the statistics that I came across. My premise was that the 4th of July holiday is more dangerous on the highways than in the streets where fireworks were being used. I also stated if he really wanted to do some community outreach, educate the public on the statistics of driving during the holiday. It may not have been the best argument and one that may not have been applicable, but it worked. I stated that there was a lot more going on during the 4th of July holiday than just fireworks. During my tenure, the city never had another person ask that fireworks be banned in Republic and subsequently, Republic continued to have one of the largest fireworks displays in the area. It was called Have-A-Blast and attracted an average of 10,000 people per year. People would come to the park for the festivities and attractions, but they would also park along the streets and highways within the city to watch the fireworks display. As other communities were cutting out any type of fireworks, Republic was being known as a place to celebrate the 4th of July.

Transition Year of 2007

2 007 was a major transition year for the city of Republic. The city had been through many changes in the past several years, including the consolidation with Brookline and going to a home rule charter, which allowed more control over the local ordinances. These two items were major actions by themselves, but to do them within a couple of years was absolutely amazing. The city administrator at the time was Dean Thompson (1994-2007). He and Mayor Collins brilliantly navigated the city through these two items. Mr. Thompson was the first city administrator in Republic history. Before 1994, the city was operated and led by the mayor and council. As anyone can imagine, this form of governance can become political very quickly. By installing a city administrator to run the day-to-day operations, the staff had one person to report to and the goal was to limit the direction given by council members to staff as had occurred in the past. Dean Thompson had actually been a council member before he was hired to be the city administrator.

In March 2007, Mr. Thompson resigned as city administrator for a position at City Utilities in Springfield, Missouri, about 8 miles to the east of Republic. Springfield had a population at the time of around 150,000 and managed their own water/sewer, gas and electric utilities, thus, the City Utilities organization. The assistant city administrator, Chris, assumed duties of the city administrator, but Chris was also the director of the planning department. Mayor Collins was more involved in the day-to-day operations than he liked and depended on Chris a little too much.

Chris was not able to watch over the planning department as needed; therefore, when the planning department would bring an item in front of council, there seemed to be more and more questions from council regarding the items. It seemed the planners were not completing their due diligence on the agenda items before submitting them for the agenda.

As council started asking more questions, the planners started to complain to Chris about the number of questions that council members were asking. At one meeting, I asked a question and the planner shot back that we were just council members and that we needed to listen to what they had to say without asking so many questions. That is paraphrased, but fairly close to the original comment. The council did not take kindly to this type of response from a staff member, especially me. Mayor Collins addressed Chris on that subject, but he kept the stance of his planners. Before the next meeting, Chris pulled me aside and told me that the planners would "lay down if the council kept questioning their presentations." They would stop or slow their work, which would hinder development and the progress of the city.

My response to his line of comments encapsulated about two sentences. The first sentence was very clear, "You and the planners do not work in a union shop and it is our job, as well as, our responsibility as council members to ensure what is brought before us is accurate." The second sentence was not so nice and to the point, "If you and the planners continue to have that mentality, then all of you will find yourselves unemployed, either now or in the future because this council will not put up with those tactics." The planners did have a change of attitude after that meeting, especially since Mayor Collins had a meeting with that entire department the following day with the same message. It did not change their opinions of council members, who they believed were ill-equipped to ask them any questions regarding their work. Interesting note, two planners left within six months of that conversation and Chris left three weeks before my first election as mayor. Timing is everything.

The summer of 2007, the city was ready to start the process of a hiring a new city administrator. The city employed an outside firm to assist in the hiring process. Mayor Collins created a committee that consisted of a few council members and a few staff members. The firm advertised for the position, collected all the resumes and filtered the resumes based on our criteria for the position. At the first meeting with the firm, the committee went through the final ten resumes and listened to the opinions of the two people from the firm that phone interviewed all the candidates. We asked questions and were in the process of narrowing our pool of candidates down to five. Once we had five, the committee would bring in all five candidates for an interview, then narrow to the final three and hold the second interview the next day. One candidate did not have a lot of municipal experience; however, he did come from a background of a family run business and had served two cities in various capacities. Mayor Collins and several other committee members dismissed his resume due to a lack of tenure in municipal government. I reviewed his resume and my thought was that he could bring a business side to the position and that would definitely be beneficial to the city as we continued to grow economically. My day job was a salesman for a large food company, so I sold the committee on taking a further look at this resume.

My comments apparently made a difference as his resume made the final five. We set a date for the meetings, interviewed all five candidates then narrowed the list to the final three after the first day. The three candidates were from diverse backgrounds. One candidate was from a community of similar size close to Joplin, Missouri. He had a finance background and seemed to be very nice. At the meet and greet the night before the second interview, he did not act as if he wanted to be involved with the city. He didn't ask any questions of our employees and seemed to only want to discuss finances. The second candidate was from a town of similar size close to St. Louis. He was very personable and experienced. The third candidate was the one that had the business background. He was very personable as well, answered all our questions and asked very detailed questions of our employees.

The next day we held the final interview with the top three. The committee interviewed all three candidates and then got together to discuss our thoughts on our choices. One interesting side note, at the end Mayor Collins had all of us stand in a circle to discuss the candidates. We had been sitting all morning interviewing and standing face-to-face with the fellow committee members was very enlightening as each of us discussed the candidates one by one without paper or phones or anything in front of us. (I would use this same tactic with our next city administrator hiring process.) When we were finished discussing the candidates, all the committee members, except one, had the same person at the top. Chris, the assistant city administrator, had the candidate with the financial background as number one. Ironically, all the other committee members had this candidate as the third candidate out of three. Chris had the list totally opposite compared to the other committee members.

The candidate that finished first was Jim Krischke, the candidate with the business background that wasn't supposed to make the first cut. He was hired and we had a few lessons learned in the process.

When it came to salary, Jim requested $1,500 more than what we had listed for the salary range and a full moving expense. The committee reconvened a few days later after the initial offer to discuss the requests and make a final decision. As the discussion commenced, Mr. Huntsinger stated that the salary is the salary and he should take it or leave it. Another committee member and council member, Keith, had an interesting rebuttal. He went around the room and asked if Jim was our number one candidate and of course everyone stated that he was the number one candidate. Keith then stated that if he is our number one candidate, then we are not going to lose him over $1,500 and some moving expenses. Discussion over, Jim was hired with the $1,500 increase and full moving expenses.

Keith brought a valuable tool to the table during that hiring process – the art of negotiation. In sales, negotiation is always prevalent. Sales are certainly at the forefront of the legal process, sales are in almost every civic organization, church and school district. Wherever there is someone attempting to get you to see it their way or to have you donate to their cause, selling is at the forefront. On the council, a spirited discussion would always bring out the inner salesperson in each council member. They would attempt to convince the others to see their point or to vote their way. The one thing that cannot happen in any organization is the personal attack or personal comments. Those do not have a place in any type of organization and are not part of the selling process. Note to all: if a person uses a personal attack or personal comment during a discussion, that person has lost all hope of convincing the others and the discussion should be ended at that moment.

The Consolidation and the Home Rule Charter

C onsolidation and annexing are two completely different avenues for communities to increase their land footprint. Annexing has a more expanded use due to the flexibility it offers with properties and the individual properties that tend to dominate the use. Annexing usually does not have to go before a full vote of the people. It can usually be done by a city council or City government. Annexation can take two forms – hostile or friendly. An example of a hostile annexation – the city would like to extend their city limits to accommodate growth and bring city services to a certain area. A landowner in the proposed area does not want city services nor do they want to be part of that city's taxing district. The city has all the other properties agreeing to the annexation (friendly) except the one homeowner (hostile). The city would have to bargain in good faith with the property owner, but in the end can force annex the property since the property is within their urban service boundary.

In certain parts of the country, cities may have an urban service boundary. This is a map boundary usually outside their city limits that could be serviced by the utilities of that city. If two communities are close, their urban service boundaries could possibly overlap, which might cause some issues as communities grow. Utilities are revenue generators for cities if they have their own. Many cities rely on franchise agreements with larger providers to bring those utilities to the community. In Republic, the city had its own water and sewer along with a franchise agreement with an electric provider and another franchise agreement with a gas company. These franchise agreements were decades old, but reviewed and renewed at certain intervals. Franchise agreements in the utility industry were basic monopolies. Whatever company was first to add their power lines or gas lines to the community, they had the upper hand on any competition. It is still this way across the county. As long as rates remain stable and service is good, the franchise agreement can be an efficient way to operate.

Consolidation is not a widely used means of expanding communities. Consolidation is basically a merger of two communities that is voted on by each community with one city ceasing their government operations and the other city assuming the governance. Navigating the legal aspect of a consolidation is extremely time consuming and rather tricky. It is best handled by experts in that municipal arena. As the city of Republic and the village of Brookline worked through the consolidation the city was represented by a member of a law firm that handled matters for the city including attending meetings. Ballot language had to be created, worded properly that would legally combine the two communities and then approved by the state before it went on the ballot to the voters. Agreements had to be created and approved that would outline the council representation process along with any other negotiated item that either community wanted. In our consolidation, Brookline wanted a park, water and sewer services along with fire and police protection.

Consolidations can happen with any two communities that are contiguous to each other. In the case of Republic and Brookline, the two city limits were next to each other on the south side of Brookline and the north east corner of Republic. The Missouri law basically stated that two communities had to be close enough to consolidate and the statute contained language describing the parameters.

The biggest hurdle on the consolidation would be the water and sewer services. In 2005, the village of Brookline was a community of 400 (est.) residents, while the city of Republic at the time was a community of 13,000 (est). The village of Brookline had a land area within its city limits that was as large as the city of Republic's land area inside its city limits. Basically, the city of Republic would double in land size and gain 400 residents. MM highway (its name) went directly through the middle of Brookline connecting two major roads – Highway 60 on the south and I-44 on the north. Both were four lanes and were the two main connecting roads to Springfield to the east. In addition to connecting the two main highways, another four-lane highway started further west off of I-44 and went diagonally across Brookline and to the south side of Springfield. It was named James River Freeway and was the fastest way for people coming to Springfield from the west to get to the south side of Springfield. Most people took this route when going to Branson, since it eliminated the 15-20 extra minutes it took by going straight down I-44 to highway 65 south to Branson.

There were two issues with putting water and sewer lines in this area. The first issue was to establish a route for the lines under the railroad tracks on the south side of Brookline and the east side of Republic. The tracks had been there before the communities and everything was built around the tracks. The tracks cut through the middle of Republic and the east side of Brookline as they went north. These tracks were an issue – if anyone has dealt with the railroad, they will know how hard it is to get a response or some semblance of cooperation from the railroads. This proved to be a major issue with the city making several attempts to gain the cooperation of the railroad. Finally, we gave up. Our solution was rather simple, we condemned the area along the tracks where our lines would go underneath and then ran the lines under the tracks. Problem solved.

The second issue encompassed running the lines underneath James River Freeway. It was not as easy as condemning property and boring underneath. With a railroad track, the distance for a bore is not that great; however, the distance to bore under a four-lane highway with a center median and wide shoulders proved to be another engineering issue. Not every citizen in the area would be attached to the water and sewer lines immediately. Part of the Brookline area was in the urban service boundary of City Utilities of Springfield; therefore, a few of the homes already had water and sewer services from Springfield. City services are almost a must for any type of industrial or retail business and the north portion of Brookline already had a business park and two more on the drawing board by the time the consolidation occurred. It was imperative that the city run the services under James River Freeway to serve the growing number of businesses in that area.

Running water and sewer lines to the main areas of Brookline was a costly endeavor, roughly estimated at 12 million dollars at the time. This was funded in a variety of ways and would be paid off over the course of several years. The services would help fund the initial upfront costs, but not completely cover those costs. Therefore, it was important to get the services in the ground and attract as many businesses as possible in the quickest manner. Established infrastructure, such as, water and sewer lines, make that community much more attractive to site selectors and commercial realtors that look for business property for their clients. By having our infrastructure in the ground and operational, our opportunity to attract business would be a step ahead of other communities that might not have the infrastructure in place but would promise to put it there if a business located there. Infrastructure can drive economic development, especially in a competitive environment. Our established infrastructure would play a big part in a highly contested development that would be looking for a new location in the next two years.

If the consolidation was not enough, Republic also embarked on a journey to become a Home Rule charter city. In the state of Missouri, most cities are fourth class cities or general rule cities indicating they have to follow the state statutes and do not have the ability to alter or change the statutes to suit their needs as a community. Home Rule Charter cities, by contrast, also had to the follow the state statutes, but had the opportunity to alter some of the statutes as needed. Becoming a Home Rule Charter was not as easy as applying to the state and getting approval. Home Rule charters basically change the way the city government operates from top to bottom. There is much more documentation that must be created, followed and kept on file. The city had to create a Home Rule committee to establish the guidelines that would be needed for the change. The committee consisted of 13 individuals and those 13 had to be voted on in a general election. The documentation that would be required was a daunting task in itself. It required an attorney that specialized in that type of municipal governance. The city had an extremely capable attorney that navigated the City through the process. Once the city officials knew exactly what would be required, the paperwork and document creation started. This was all done before the charter could be presented before the state for approval.

While all the background work was being completed, Mayor Collins started a public relations campaign to educate the community on the Home Rule Charter and convince the citizens to vote for it. The documents cleared the state and Republic was approved to go to the voters for approval. The campaign worked as well. The vote passed the citizens and Republic became a Home Rule Charter city. At the time, there were approximately 955 incorporated cities in the state of Missouri. 911 were general rule or fourth-class cities. Republic became one of the 38 cities that were Home Rule Charter cities. The overall governance of Republic had not changed much with the passing of the Home Rule charter, but the city now had the ability to make changes to its policies, create and establish new policies and be more in control of how it operated. The Home Rule charter definitely established Republic as a progressive community and one that looked toward the future.

Another important event that happened in 2007 was the ice storm. This incident happened a few days after the January closing date of sign-up in the city for the April election. A horrendous ice storm hit the entire southwest Missouri region. Ice had covered everything in a thick crystallized beauty. The ice came down and stuck to the roads, the homes, the sidewalks, the brown grass in the yards and of course it stuck to the power lines. Power was out everywhere in the region with very few people having any type of supplied power. As trees broke, power lines fell and basically southwest Missouri went dark. For some, the power remained out for seven days. The clean-up was going to be a major project all over the area, especially in Republic. Clean-up started almost immediately before the power returned. City crews were working on clearing the fallen trees from roadways and free any power lines that were being hindered by debris.

The power was eventually restored in intervals around the area. All cities were doing the same thing cleaning up as much debris as possible. It was an overwhelming task for any city. Most crews were not able to keep up with the debris piling up beside the roadways. Citizens were instructed to take all their debris and pile it in front of their homes. A truck eventually would be by to collect it. Trees were down in almost every yard that had one, small ones and large ones, not one tree was immune to the ice carnage. Like all cities in the area, the city of Republic was having a difficult time collecting all the debris with the most difficult task of where to put all the debris. We decided to go out for bid for a company or a set of companies to collect the debris, haul it and find a suitable home that was legal. It is amazing how some companies will skirt the law to increase their profits. At a council meeting shortly after receiving the bids, the council selected a company. The mayor opened the floor for the winning company to discuss any questions the council might have regarding the project. This is where things got a little out of hand. Competing companies were in attendance and when the company was selected, the company representatives of the companies that were not selected became very vocal in their disapproval.

At one point, a company representative made a very loud disparaging comment about the winning company, which caused the winning company representative to verbally retaliate as he stood at the podium to answer questions from council. Apparently, debris hauling is a hotly contested business with very few of these men not having a good thing to say about the others. That comment by the winner and another comment by another company started a barrage of comments between all combatants. Representatives from the non-selected companies were attacking each other, not just the winner. The comments ranged from rather funny to downright scathing. It was happening so fast and the comments were so quick, it was hard to log any of them, however one comment rather summed it up for me. The comments were getting personal, very personal to these men, but one of the last comments made was from a losing bidder to another losing bidder, not even to the winning bidder. It was almost as junior high as it could get. He said, and this is paraphrased, "Yea, but at least my trucks don't leak oil all over God's creation. You leave enough oil everywhere you go to keep the oil companies in business. I should follow you around and collect the oil for my truck." And so, the meeting went on like that for a few minutes until Mayor Collins got a handle on the situation. We selected a company and the debris removal commenced the next day.

Our family was on vacation in Florida at the time of the ice storm. We were warm, had electricity and "had" to stay an extra day due to all the flights to Springfield being cancelled. It was a tough way to spend the time when everyone back home in Republic was out of power. Found out later, that our subdivision was on the same grid as the electric company's local office, therefore our subdivision had power before anyone else in town. The electric company restored power to their office as soon as possible. They needed the building as a local command center to coordinate their power restoring activities. Our untimely and unplanned absence from the ice storm was the first of a few times when we were out of town during emergency events.

Running for Mayor

At the April election cycle in 2007, I ran again for the ward 3 council position. Like the first time, I was out of town during the sign up time frame. This time, I was the incumbent but my position on the ballot changed slightly. Instead of being second on the ballot, I was actually third on the ballot. There were two others that were running against me. Neither had been involved with the City in any capacity that we knew about, but both had signed up to run for the position. My campaign consisted of the same white signs with red lettering and the same wooden stakes hammered in the ground with a sledgehammer. The signs were stapled to the wooden stakes – one on each side. Since my signs were only one sided, it took two signs to be read front and back or read both ways from the street. With only 65 signs, there were only 32 opportunities to put the back-to-back signs in locations around the ward. The extra sign was used in reserve in case we had a sign destroyed or run over by a mower.

We located about 20 signs along the two main streets leading to the community center. The remaining signs were put in various locations within the ward. Three signs were put in the common area behind the fences of our subdivision where my Burma-Shave sign went at the 2005 election. This location caused some issues within our subdivision this time around. The area was actually common area for our subdivision and maintained by the subdivision owner Matt Henry. Matt lived right behind us. We shared a fence and become good friends over the years. He gave me permission to put the signs in that location.

However, a homeowner in that area was not a fan of political signs. She complained that the sign behind her fence gave the impression that they were supporting me in the election. Her complaint also stated that it gave the appearance that the entire subdivision was supporting me. The complainant literally lived a block from us and directly across from the neighborhood pool. We had never met. Matt, who lived behind us, was about 500 feet from their front door. It was small subdivision with fewer than 100 houses at that time.

Matt discussed the complaint with me and we agreed to remove the signs from the common area. He thought they were okay, but knew this person would not give up until they were removed. Therefore, the signs were removed. A few days later at our neighborhood pool, a neighbor that lived two houses over from the complainant, inquired why my signs were gone. I explained the situation and did not divulge the person that made the complaint. The neighbor made the comment that the fences were private property and asked me to put a sign on their fence. Two other neighbors that lived on the other side of the complainant requested a sign as well. We set up a time for the signs to be stapled to the fence. The next day, we stapled three signs to their fences with them supervising the installation.

It did not take long for Matt to receive another call. The same person made the same argument and requested the same result. This time, Matt told her the signs were placed at her neighbor's request since it was their fence. He went on to tell her that she had every right to put a political sign on her fence, but all signs in the common area were now banned. The election was a month away and we didn't have any trouble with signs from that point moving forward.

The day of the election had an interesting twist. Scott Lowery was running against me on the ballot had a friend that was on the city council. That friend was Chad Cole. Chad was elected in ward IV and sat beside me on council. He was on council when Mayor Collins had the infamous "Shut-up, Shut-up" comment. After the incident in open session, Chad requested that Mayor Collins apologize to the council members and the audience. I agreed with him and Mayor Collins did somewhat apologize. The morning of the election, I had run an errand early and was on my way back to the house. Our subdivision was directly across from the community center where our ward voted. As I turned into our subdivision, out in front of the community center, Chad was waving a sign and waving at people. The sign said, "Vote for Lowery, Ward 3". I was rather shocked to see a sitting council member campaigning against a person that he sat next to on the council. We never had any major disagreements and had voted differently on a variety of issues, but it was business to me and it was my hope it was business with him as well. Whatever his motives, he was going to be there all day campaigning.

Upon arriving home, my phone rang and it was David Pittman my campaign manager. He told me he had permission from one more homeowner for a sign and they were on the main street to the community center. I tossed my last sign in the car with the stake and the sledgehammer and headed out the door. It was still breakfast time and I was hungry. On my way out of the subdivision, I stopped and asked Chad if he was hungry and that I would buy breakfast from McDonald's if he wanted something. I was headed there after adding the sign anyway. He politely declined, albeit a bit sheepishly after having spoken with me. The sign was added and I proceeded to

McDonald's.   Not only did I purchase myself
something, I purchased Chad something as well.   I
stopped by and told him I had breakfast if he wanted it,
since we both had the same thing. He declined again,
but at least he knew I wasn't upset about having him
campaign against me.

My first council run in 2005 was against an
incumbent and I was second on the ballot. This second
run for the council was against two others and I was
third on the ballot this time with a sitting council
member campaigning against me at the polling
location. The result was an interesting one. I won 201-
91-51-4.   The 4 were write-in candidates.   That
indicates there are 4 people with a sense of humor
during election time. It was a larger margin of victory
than my first election in 2005.

Later in 2007, Mayor Collins had asked me if he
stepped down from the mayoral position, would I be
running for mayor. It wasn't so much a question as it
was him letting me know he was not going to run again.
This was also the same time that he decided to run for
the 134th district state representative position. I had
not really thought about running for mayor, but always
knew that if it were me in that position, things would
be done differently in certain areas of the city. I ran the
idea of running for mayor by my wife, Diane. Her one-
word answer was "no". I didn't test it any further; the
two word answer may come out at that point "no no".
My wife was born in Springfield and had moved to
Republic when she was 8 years old. She had lived in
Republic or Springfield her entire life. When I ran the
first time for council, she said that Republic has always
been a political town and that people that didn't grow
up there or were from other places found it difficult to
get on any type of civic organization, city or school.
Almost verbatim of what Mayor Collins told me. After

being on city council for two years (2005-2007), I had established some type of rapport with the local community. My thought was that we had made progress in those three years and that I could make a difference by being mayor.

The sign up date for the April, 2008 election started the first week of December, 2007 and went through the second week of January, 2008. Diane knew that it was coming up and she told me she really did not want me running for mayor. I never said too much to that point, but always thought I could make a difference, so on the first sign-up day, I went down to city hall and signed up to run for mayor. At the time, I was in the middle of my two-year council seat term. If elected mayor, my council seat in ward 3 would be vacated, if nobody ran, I would appoint a member to council for the one year until the next election. At sign up, the city clerk gives everyone a packet of information with the council position in which they signed up, labeled on the front. That packet went right to the passenger seat of the car after sign up. The only issue with the packet being in that location was that I would inevitably forget about it. This was my third time to sign up for a municipal election and knew what was in the packet, since the city clerk reviewed it as we were signing on the dotted line to run for the positions. That evening, I went to pick up Diane from work and totally forgot about the packet. She got in the car and saw the packet. She looked at me and said, "What is this? I thought we talked about this?" The only thing that came to mind was my thought all along. I said, "But I feel I can make a difference." It was a quiet ride that evening, but the music was so good on the radio.

The last day of sign up came and went without anyone else signing up for the mayoral position. I would be running unopposed. Running unopposed was something that I was not used to in an election and something the mayor position was certainly not used to. Since Mayor Collins was concentrating on his state representative campaign and was not running again, I basically became the interim mayor even as mayor pro tem. The city administrator would call the mayor and then call to update me during the transition time between the first week of January and the election in April.

It did not take long for a small crisis to hit the city. In January, 2008, the sign up for the city offices had closed. Running unopposed was unique in the city of Republic. The mayor position had been a coveted position in the years before and not having to campaign has its advantages. At the end of that week, a tornado hit the city, a very rare occurrence in January. The tornado hit in the early evening during a vicious series of thunderstorms. The tornado touched down on the north side of Republic and took off part of the roof at an elementary school and knocked out power around the community, which limited communication. Most of the information at the time of the incident was being funneled to the city administrator and he was passing along the information to Mayor Collins and me. With Mayor Collins concentrating on his campaign and me running unopposed, my time as mayor had basically started. It did not start with me in town during the tornado incident nor did it start with Mayor Collins in town. He was out of town and not answering his phone. The city administrator knew where both of us were located and had both our cell phone numbers.

My family and I were at the airport attempting to fly to Florida for our vacation. My parents had a place there during the winter and we would travel there to take a nice warm winter vacation. While at the airport in Springfield, a tornado warning sounded and everyone had to leave the terminal and return to the main concourse away from the windows. It also was on the other side of security; therefore, everyone had to maneuver through security again and that put a small delay in all the flights. After making it through security, we were herded into the plane as fast as possible. We soon found out why we were being ushered into the plane so quickly. The pilot came on the intercom after everyone was on and told us that there was a small chance to get off the ground in between two storm cells. The second storm apparently had some potential rotation in it. Since the storm was moving from southwest to northeast and our plane would be flying east/southeast, we had a small chance to get in the air and move in the opposite direction of the storm. Everyone in the plane got seated as fast as possible. No one wanted to disembark, go back the main concourse and start the process over.

The pilot pushed away from the gate and in a very short time we were airborne. We could see a storm on our left and a storm on our right as we lifted into the sky. From my seat, I could see the storm that was likely hitting Republic at that moment and noticed lots of lightening and very dark clouds. I did not know anything that was going on at that time, but when we landed, we would know the full extent of the situation.

Two hours later, we landed in Florida and once my phone was powered on, it blew up with text messages and missed calls. The city administrator had texted me a barrage of information as they uncovered the mess at the school. There were several missed calls with messages outlining the situation as well. We exited baggage claim, put our luggage into my parents car and I started checking the voicemail and reading the texts. I called the city administrator to get an update. He stated the tornado had removed part of the elementary school roof and there were people inside at the time. No one was injured and everyone made it out safely after the storm had passed. After several minutes of debriefing, I understood the situation in Republic was under control. We planned to talk the next day for an update. We calculated the time of the tornado was about the same time as our plane was lifting off the ground. Since the airport was around 14 miles away from the school and the tornado was apparently happening as we took off, there was no way that the airport or pilots would have known about that storm cell. Additionally, this was not to be the last encounter we would have with tornados in our community or in southwest Missouri.

During the call with the city administrator the next day, he informed me that it was not a large tornado, but a smaller one that touched down in the city. He briefed me on the clean-up efforts and how the city and the school were working together. In the past, the school and city worked together; however, it was not the best situation between the two entities. It was a good thing that we were working together on this one, but sad that it took a tragedy of this type to bring people together. So, this was the second time that we had been out of town during a storm related event. The city administrator joked that every time I would take vacation to Florida in January, something always happens in the city. Ironically, he was right as the years passed.

Starting Down the Path of Change

The April, 2008, election was rather uneventful, although the first meeting after the election was an interesting one. This would be the last meeting with five wards and ten council members. The Brookline consolidation agreement stated that Brookline would have a ward for them with two members. This was to last through the April election in 2008. Ward V, the Brookline ward, would be rolled in to Ward I and the council would return to four wards and eight members. Another interesting item at the meeting surrounded Mayor Collins; this was his last meeting as mayor. He would step down after all old business was finished, but it was not after some spirited discussion. One old business item on the agenda was a potential pay raise for the council members. Another old business item was the awarding of the city's third-party engineering contract. This had the potential to become a hotly discussed item. Those two items generated some interesting discussion and a vote that would help move a city and a company forward.

The newly elected officials were sworn-in at the first meeting immediately after the election, however they were only sworn in after old business was conducted and concluded by the council. This was to ensure that the council members leaving would have an opportunity to vote and finish any business started when they were on the council. It also ensured the newly elected members would not have to vote on an item in which they possibly would not have any knowledge. Old business was conducted first with the current line-up of the ten council members. Due to the election of new members and the last meeting for other members, we held the council meeting at the community center and the council chamber was rather full that night. The engineering firms that vied for the third-party contract were also in attendance. The local media were there as well, due to Mayor Collins last meeting along with some possible fireworks on the agenda items.

The agenda item on the pay raise brought a spirited discussion. A board could not give themselves a raise during the year. They could vote to give the next set of members a pay raise, though. In our situation, council members were paid one hundred dollars per month to serve and the mayor paid two hundred dollars per month to serve. This was not much money due to the time spent at council meetings, special meetings, events and functions while representing the city. There are many councils and boards that do not pay anything to serve. The proposal would double the payments, therefore the council members would receive two hundred dollars a month and the mayor would receive four hundred dollars a month. On a yearly basis it was $2,400 for the council members and $4,800 for the mayor. Since my swearing in as the new mayor was after the old business, the pay raise would be affecting me along with other council members that either stayed on council or new to council. The discussion was good with some excellent points being voiced. My comments were not in favor of the proposal. I stated that my service was just that, service. I volunteered for the council and then was elected without knowing that a council position actually paid. The money was not why I signed up and certainly was not my reason for becoming mayor. I voted against the resolution but it passed.

The engineering item on the agenda that night would help define a few things moving forward. It was to award the third-party engineering contract. Most all cities have third party engineering companies on retainer for a variety of reasons. They review plats submitted, review engineering on projects, do engineering on projects and work very close to the public works department, planning department and economic development department. They also consult with the city on projects or proposed projects to help assist the city in ensuring the projects are engineered properly. This is to ensure that any prejudice is removed by having an unbiased third party review projects. This keeps the city safe from any type of lawsuit of unfair requirements or biased reviews. The third party engineering contracts are important to the engineering firms since it basically gives them an inside track to other more lucrative engineering project contracts within the city. It also gives them the upper hand on engineering contracts when it comes to information on companies that are planning on relocating to the city. They can use their contacts at the city as a selling point to potential companies.

The city went out for bid for the third party engineer contract. This was rather unusual for the city since they had awarded the bid to the same firm for many years, Scott Consulting, without a formal bidding process. This was allowed under certain regulations within the city but was not the most transparent way to conduct business. Jim, the new city administrator, decided that the best way to be more transparent was to go out for bid and I was behind it all the way. Three firms had submitted bids and made presentations to a committee established by Mayor Collins. The committee reviewed all the information and then recommended a winner to the council, but it was still up to the council to decide the winner. At the council meeting the three firms could make a presentation to the full council. All the presentations were good and all could do whatever we needed as a city. During the discussion, questions were asked of each firm and answers given.

The awarding of the engineering contract would be the last vote under Mayor Collins. As the vote went around the table, the vote was tied 5-5 with Scott Consulting and one other firm. This meant that Mayor Collins provided the last vote to break the tie. Mayor Collins did not have many votes in his tenure that broke ties. This was his last vote and would affect the city for three more years, since the contract was a three-year contract. Three years that Mayor Collins would not be associated with the city, but three years that would have me involved for at least two of those years, since our terms were two-year terms. My vote was for another firm and not for Scott Consulting. Mayor Collins knew my preference for an engineering firm that would be under my leadership at the city. He knew that Scott Consulting did a good job for him under his tenure; therefore he was at a crossroads. Vote for the firm that the new mayor wanted or vote for the firm that did a good job for him and show some loyalty to Scott Consulting. He voted for Scott Consulting and broke the tie. That was his last official duty as mayor and he stepped down gracefully.

The council was back to eight members with me leading from the mayor position from that point forward. I do not remember much about the first meeting. I do remember a very concerned person in the audience. That person was the Scott Consulting representative that had been the city's third-party engineer for the better part of 20 years, John Forrester. John was a very nice man and had worked with the city for many years. He was concerned that the newly elected mayor did not vote for his firm on a contract renewal. This made John extremely concerned since many of our outside contracts went to Scott Consulting. The very next day after the meeting, John called the city administrator first thing in the morning very upset about the vote and my stance toward his firm. He wanted to meet with me and the city administrator. We scheduled a meeting for the very next day in the city administrator's office.

The meeting with John went as expected. John voiced his concern over my stance and proceeded to tell me about all the past work that he and Scott Consulting had completed for the city and that my vote did not show loyalty to all that work. That is a short synopsis of that part of the discussion. When John asked our opinion, Jim the city administrator, told him the rationale for going out for bid. We, as a city, needed to be more transparent in all our transactions and actions as a council. It looked like favoritism by not going out for bid on the third-party contract and it was in the best interest of the tax payer money to ensure we were being billed fairly. Jim explained this and told John that the old way of doing business was not going to fly with him or me moving forward. John then pointed the questions in my direction. John did not know how to ask me why I voted the way that I did. He would ask a series of questions hoping for my thoughts on the subject. Most of the questions Jim would answer, since he had to work with the third-party engineer on a weekly basis, if necessary. Being in sales allows me the opportunity to talk and that opportunity could certainly be acted upon in the municipal government setting. For those of you that do not know me and for some that do know me, there are times to talk and times to listen. One thing about situations like this one, listening and not saying anything can put one at a great advantage. Most people do not like silence when having a conversation; therefore, they will continue to talk even when it may be your turn to talk. Listening was the one thing that I did the most as mayor. Listen first, talk second, unless the situation required talking first which usually meant that the mayor was supposed to talk first. By listening first and at times not saying anything in return, the person talking would usually say enough to hang themselves. This proved very effective in disciplinary actions and in listening to proposals.

John finally got around to asking me about my vote and really wanted to know why I had voted against his firm. Now, by this time, John had almost talked himself into a hole and Jim threw him a lifeline almost every time, but it was my time to talk and it was short and sweet. I told John that he stood in front of that council and told us everything he and his firm had done for the city of Republic over his tenure at the city. I stated that the other firms had told us what they would do for the city over the next three years. The city of Republic was going to be moving forward and we already knew what he had done for us, we were looking forward to what he was going to do for us over the next three years. In other words, John tried to sell his past success with us in hopes that it would gain our loyalty again and award him the contact. We were looking forward to the future and I told him we already knew what he had done for us and that was in the past. If he could not improve and get better as a third party engineer, then we as a city could not move forward at the pace that we wanted. John understood completely, but that would not be the last issue we had with the third party engineer.

A few months later, Jim and I were talking about the Brookline water/sewer line project and he mentioned the number and amount of change orders to the project. Most of these had to come before city council for approval and had been approved in the past. These caught my eye, as they were substantial amounts, roughly $50,000. I instructed Jim to go back and review all the contracts and start looking into the change order amounts the city was receiving. As a council member, I remember approving a few change fees. It always seemed that it was an oversight or an unforeseen event that caused the change orders. In the case of the roughly $50,000 in change fees, something was just not right. Change orders are basically a re-work of the engineering contractual services. Once an engineering firm wins a bid, they prepare the engineering documents for the project. The documents or plans should encompass the entire project start to finish without changes or a small change every now and then. Change orders generally are to the contractor performing the work on the project and not necessarily to the engineering fees although that does occur.

Not everything can be foreseen in a set of plans that an engineer creates, especially on big projects. Smaller projects should not have any, especially if the project is the specialty of the engineering firm. Many change orders were encountered due to the upfront work not being thorough enough. Our goal was to analyze our change orders and implement procedures to ensure our project planning improved. The end result should be a reduction in change orders. Jim started analyzing our projects and any change orders that were listed.

What Jim found on our projects was rather alarming. We had a dilemma on our hands. Our projects appeared to have the right engineering and yet we had way too many change orders. Our change orders seem to be prevalent in almost all our projects. The water/sewer lines in Brookline just brought to light a larger issue that needed to be addressed. We had to create a solution, so Jim and I sat down to discuss our alternatives. First, we had to identify the issue or if there really was an issue with change orders. Jim's analysis did exactly that as it identified a pattern of change orders. Next, we had to create a solution that would solve the issue for the short term and long term. After that, we had to create a plan of action and identify the individuals that were going to be involved with making the changes. Once we had the plan of action and the individuals that were part of the solution, we would then institute the plan and get the individuals involved with goals that were actionable and accountable.

There are several ways to deal with change orders. First, ensure that the bid documents created by the city were all encompassing with nothing forgotten. Second, build into the contract a no-change fee clause or a limited change orders clause. Usually, these were based on a percentage of the contract cost or set limited amount. This would limit the city's liability regarding cost and would ensure that the engineering firm did their complete due diligence. We identified that David the public works director and John from Scott Consulting would be the two individuals that were held accountable for the positive change. Jim met with David and explained the direction we were taking. Jim did not tell all that was said, but David agreed to work on reducing the number of change orders. Jim wanted to meet with John and asked that I attend the meeting. We were going to discuss the change orders and how the third-party engineer was going to be a part of the process for a positive change.

In the discussion with John, he indicated that he went along with David on many, not all, of the projects issues because he was afraid that David would recommend that the city use another firm. John did not want to lose the business after all those years. I approached this with an attitude that I learned many years before, "If it's not broke, break it". John was still living in the past and our goal as a city was to move forward. We told John that we cannot move forward with him not standing up to David on these issues. We instilled in John that we would be holding David and him accountable for all change orders and any other issues that seem to arise on the contracts that come before the council. In other words, John needed to take charge, ensure the job was done correctly and look out for the interests of the city. If Scott Consulting took care of their business, the engineering contracts would take care of themselves and Scott Consulting could concentrate on the future of the city along with the city council. John agreed but was somewhat reluctant at first. He did not want to jeopardize his long-standing friendship with David, but at the same time knew things were going to change either with Scott Consulting or without Scott Consulting. John wanted to be a part of the future of Republic and stepped up his role within the city.

Change orders were reduced immediately and the city did not have an issue from that point to the end of my tenure. Likewise, Scott Consulting (now Olssen engineering through a merger) was still the city's third party engineer when I left in August, 2016. This was not without issues between David and John over the years, but business is business.

The Three Puzzle Pieces

Running for Mayor would not have occurred if there were not three people already in place. Jim Krischke was the first person. He was hired as the City Administrator and we seemed to work well together during the short time he was city administrator and I was on the council in Ward 3. Jim brought a business background to the city government and had the same vision as me. That vision was economic growth. It was a rather vague vision and did not contain any type of mission or goals. It was plainly economic growth. That encompassed many different areas around the city to make it more marketable. Public works had to be willing to find ways to make projects work on the infrastructure side to attract companies that would be using the city services. This was not a blank check nor did it allow for anything outside of the city codes. It did focus their attention on making projects work in a manner in which business would find it easy to do business with the city. This was successful part of the time and unsuccessful the other part.

The vision encompassed the planning department to find creative solutions to the some of the planning issues that always seem to appear in the planning process. They had to be ready to make decisions and not get bogged down in the "what if" statements that stalemate so many projects. One of my comments to the planning department stated that they could "what if" things to death, but in the end, they had to make a decision moving forward. Besides, as the experts they are charged with overcoming the "what if" statements.

In other words, don't tell me why something cannot be done; tell me what we need to do in order to overcome it. Economic growth was going to happen and it was up to us to ensure it was properly managed growth. The planning department was instrumental in fulfilling that portion of economic growth.

Additionally, the vision of economic growth would encompass every department. The police would need to demonstrate that we had a safe, friendly community to attract the families that would be accompanying the new business. The fire department had to demonstrate a proactive approach to fire safety and a short response time when they were needed. The parks department had to continue with innovative programs and upgrade the parks system at every opportunity. This would outwardly show that Republic was a progressive community and a great place to call home.

Economic growth is a systemic process. Every department was involved with the vision of economic growth directly or indirectly. In my opinion, all were an integral part of a successful community driving economic growth. Jim and I viewed the vision the same along with the role that every department would have in the economic growth process. It could be that Jim agreed with my vision and went along with it due to the mayor/city administrator relationship. In my opinion Jim believed the same way as me and that is why it worked so well for so long.

The second person that had to be in place was Brenda Jackson the city clerk. Brenda had worked for the city of Springfield in the police department for many years. We found out after she was hired that her husband Pepper Jackson was a Springfield police officer and had worked with my brother-in-law. Brenda and Pepper were very nice people. Brenda was the most organized person I have ever met. She worked for the council and reported to the council. During the day-to-day operations she reported to the city administrator. Brenda was hired in 2005 and came through an interesting interview with Mayor Collins, Dean Thompson the city administrator at the time, Jim Huntsinger the mayor pro-tem along with me. During the interview, we were firing questions to Brenda that we had written for ourselves. She was answering them with her opinions and thoughts without hesitation. Mayor Collins was known for going off script every now and then with that interview being one of those moments. Mayor Collins asked Brenda if she was married and did she have any kids, both clearly inappropriate questions. In total shock, I looked down toward the Mayor and saw Dean's face in disbelief in the process. It was one of those moments when you drop the milk out of the refrigerator. You drop it and then you see it fall knowing there is going to be a big mess when it lands. This was one of those moments. The Mayor's question was like the milk falling and there was not really anything to do except brace for the mess. Jim Huntsinger quickly told her she did not have to answer those questions, since they were not appropriate. Brenda was very gracious about it and answered the questions without giving too much detail.

Brenda was in the Mayor's office on a daily basis. All calls or emails or mail for the Mayor went to her for processing. Every item that comes to the city for the mayor was stamped with the date it was received. This eliminated any confusion on when something arrived. As with most staff members when they are around the mayor, they do not give their opinion very often for whatever reason. Brenda would offer her opinion to me when asked and at times when unsolicited. It was always appreciated, even when we disagreed about something. She always would end her opinions with the same phrase, "You are the mayor and you can do what you want." She understood the mayor role and understood her role in the governance of the city. Brenda retired from the city in 2019 and I attended her retirement dinner at her last council meeting. I was in the Springfield area on business and planned it around her retirement, although I texted her that evening letting her know how much I appreciated her over my tenure and how sad I was not being able to attend her retirement. When I showed up before the meeting, the room was almost full. As soon as I entered the room, she blurted out, "The mayor's here! You texted me you were not able to make it". We hugged and I told her I would not miss it for anything. During the meeting, the council allowed me to read a prepared statement that I had written. Part of that statement reiterated that I would not have run for mayor unless she was the city clerk.

The third person that had to be in place for me to run for Mayor was Ron Dirickson, the city attorney. Ron had worked in the business world for Burroughs Corporation and Conoco Energy. After going to law school, Ron got into municipal government law work while in private practice and then at the city of Springfield for 10 years. Ron was from Oklahoma and we hit it off, even though I was from Kansas. The Sooner jokes and Kansas jokes were constantly being lobbed between the two of us. I had the upper hand since he was an attorney and there seems to be an endless supply of lawyer jokes. One of my favorite ones to tell Ron or to anyone around when Ron was with me was the joke about the attorney and the godfather. What do you get when you mix an attorney and a godfather? A person that will make you an offer you can't understand. Ron was always a good sport about it and we had a few good jabs over the years. The one thing about Ron that always impressed me was the fact that we could be having a conversation and he would always listen to all points being made regardless of whether he agreed with them or did not agree with them.

Ron was hired in June of 2005 shortly after the consolidation and it immediately paid off for the city. The city had been paying for legal services over the years and being billed by the job. Any call or request for opinion was billed to the city along with attending council meetings and any other function that required an attorney. In 2004/2005, the city paid a little over $90,000 in legal services for legal firm representation that was not full time. The decision was made to hire a full-time attorney and pay them around that number. It was worth every penny. We were able to have full time legal services and consult with the attorney before moving forward with contracts, legal documents and a host of other items.

One other item that impressed me about Ron was his demeanor in a council meeting. Many attorneys on councils tend to try and run the meeting or interject on everything said. Ron was very quiet and only gave his opinion when asked. He would occasionally interject when the council would be "chasing rabbits". The Sunshine Law stated that we could not discuss something that was not on the posted agenda. When the council discussion got outside the agenda lines, Ron would bring it back to a point where the council was on task again. He would do this in a variety of ways. At times he would interrupt and let everyone know we were off topic; other times he would lean over and let me know we were off topic or on the verge of being off topic in which I would stop the discussion and bring it back on topic. At one meeting Ron drew something on a piece of paper and slid it front of me, since he sat next to me on my right. The first time he did it, I thought he was bored and just doodling; therefore, I did not pay much attention to it. He then nudged me and pointed at the picture. I still could not tell what it was, so we kept going. Finally, he nudges me, pointed at the drawing and said we are chasing rabbits. I said that was fine and would bring the conversation back but had to ask him what was on that piece of paper. He said it was a rabbit and we were chasing them. To me, it resembled a rabbit, maybe around the ears. Looked more like a donkey. That was the most enjoyable way Ron would attempt to bring the conversation back to the agenda when he would attempt to draw a rabbit on a piece of paper. Great attorney, poor doodler.

Those three individuals had to be in place for me to run for mayor. It was imperative to have good leadership in the city administrator position, in-house legal services and a city clerk that was extremely organized. These three people and their abilities allowed me to be comfortable enough to run for mayor. If one of the three had not been in place, I would not have run for mayor. It must be said that my thoughts about running for mayor only surfaced when Mayor Collins told me he was not going to run for mayor again, but for the state position. That was in 2007 well after all three of them were on board at the city.

Side story: An attorney's best friend. City Hall was a conglomeration of three different buildings that were somehow fused together to create one large building with multiple access points, offices in strange locations and bathrooms in odd places. One building was an insurance office; another was just an office and the other portion an old bank. The vault is still there and used for storage. This meant that there was really no logical layout for most of the offices there. Ron

Dirickson's office was a former small conference room in the back that had been turned into two small offices with a hallway in between going to the back. The old building always had issues with rainwater leakage, bugs and just general maintenance. That happens when the buildings are old and modern modifications fail to address any of the major issues. One day, Ron was sitting in his office working at his desk and noticed little white things floating down on to his desk. Ron did not think too much of it due to the maintenance workers in the building doing something above the ceiling tiles. He thought it might be insulation or loose pieces of the ceiling tiles. The white floating objects were not too bad that day and did not mention anything to the maintenance workers. The next day, Ron came in and found his desk, the floor, the computer, his chair and basically everything in the office covered in white objects. Those little white objects just happened to be termites. Apparently, the maintenance workers were in the ceiling above the tiles working and the termites became disturbed. As all disturbed termites do, they sought out an attorney. Ron didn't have an office after his termite infestation and there were not any offices available; therefore, I volunteered my Mayor's office to Ron and we would find me a new office, but probably not the termite laden one. This started a series of office relocations for me while at the city.

A Very Interesting First Year

One of my very first acts as mayor was to rearrange the agenda. In our form of government, the mayor really controlled one item at a council meeting other than running the meeting and breaking ties. That one item was the agenda. The mayor could choose not to add a topic to the agenda or to choose to add one. If a council member had a topic that they wanted on the agenda and the mayor did not want it on the agenda, then the council member would need two other council members to sign a request letter for that topic to be added to the agenda. This was a good check and balance for a city government as it kept the agenda straight forward.

Under Mayor Collins, the agenda contained ordinances, resolutions and discussion items. Ordinances required two readings at different council meetings, while resolutions were discussed and voted on during the same meeting. Discussion topics were items that the Mayor or staff would put on the agenda to obtain councils thoughts and potentially give them direction. My first act was to remove discussion items from the agendas. The council was there to make decisions on agenda items brought before them. The staff members are the experts and need to bring forward items that need an approval from council. By discussing the items first, the staff may not make the best decision when they return with the ordinance or resolution. They may have created the ordinance or resolution with their thought of what council wants, as opposed to what is needed. It was the job of staff to ensure any ordinance or resolution had been thoroughly reviewed without prejudice. Obtaining the best ordinance or resolution was the goal and not just to get something passed. Staff members could not be afraid of having something rejected by council. They had to keep focus on accuracy and ensuring the right ordinance or resolution was in front of council.

An old phrase seemed to sum up some of the ordinances and resolutions that we were seeing in the meetings; "If you do what you've always have done, you get what you've always got." Poor grammar, but it was applicable. The discussion items were influencing the future ordinances and resolutions and we were not getting the best out of the staff members. In this situation, we needed to change the agenda and create what we needed to move forward. So, we removed discussion items from the agenda. We had already established that each council member could meet with the city administrator once a month; therefore, the discussion items could take place during those meetings and not on a public agenda.

Staff members enjoyed this new agenda without the discussion items and the newfound freedom it gave them to do their job to the best of their ability without council interference. The agenda was not broken, however it was certainly not effective when it came to the discussion items. I employed one of the other phrases picked up in my business life; "If it's not broke, break it." In order to make things better, we sometimes need to break the old way of doing something and create a better way of doing it. One additional thought on discussion items on council agendas. Discussion is usually where meetings get off track very quickly. Many meetings have gone into the ditch due to items being discussed where nothing will be voted on or acted on during that time. If someone is going to have a meeting, set the agenda, stick to the agenda and if any potential non-agenda discussion items become present, add those to the next meeting's agenda then move on to the next item.

This also applies to any business-related meeting as well. Many business meetings get side-tracked with discussions that are not pertinent to the topic being discussed. There are a variety of reasons that people bring up items not necessarily on topic. It takes a strong leader to recognize the group is off-task and bring the discussion back to topic. A leader is more like a judge than an attorney. The judge listens to all sides of the discussion, keeps the discussion on task and interjects when necessary. The "when necessary" is a fine line and a point that some leaders do not understand. Many leaders think they are there to impart their wisdom or direction to a group of individuals. Leadership requires listening more than speaking.

Another one of my first acts as mayor was to create a group of individuals that would meet once a month and have topics on a variety of subjects. Once these were discussed, they would be included on each subsequent agenda until they were fully resolved. This group was called the PAR Group. PAR stood for Planning and Review. The group consisted of the city administrator, finance director, city attorney, public works director, planning/economic development director, the city's third party engineer, the mayor pro tem, the city administrator's executive assistant and the mayor. The PAR group was designed to fully review topics ranging from public works projects to intergovernmental relationships. If the topic needed some in depth review and vetted opinions, the PAR group was the place to discuss it. The first agenda covered about 10 items including the water/sewer project in Brookline, which was not going as planned.

Connie, the city administrator's assistant, would take the notes at the PAR group meeting and she did it in shorthand. I never understood how she could accurately quote me and the others with a few squiggly lines that looked somewhat better than Ron's rabbit "drawings" at the council meetings. At one particular PAR group meeting, I was absent and that was not a good thing for this meeting. The city was having issues with installing the water/sewer lines in the Brookline area of Republic. This was part of the 12 million dollar infrastructure improvements that were part of the Brookline consolidation. The issue seemed to be the lack of initiative from the public works director and the third party engineer to find a solution with the contractor for boring under James River Freeway to run the lines. It appeared that they were delaying the project for whatever reason without any real solutions being targeted. Connie sent out the minutes from the meeting and since I was out of town during the meeting, the minutes were going to be thoroughly read. What I saw in the minutes alarmed me. We still did not have any solutions for the issue and there was a comment in the minutes regarding three potential solutions, but they had to be reviewed and the engineers look at them to see if they were even viable before a decision could be made. It seemed that no one wanted to make a decision. The third party engineer did not want to, our public works director didn't want to and neither did the contractor that was hired to do the work. There seemed to be some dispute with the contractor, the third party engineer and our public works director.

In one of my not so fine moments, I chose to hit reply to all on the minutes with my limited comments. Granted, we had discussed solutions and I thought we were headed correctly with the direction given at the prior PAR meeting, but that was not the case. First lesson here, never send an email in anger. Second lesson, type the email in anger but never address the email. Third lesson, sleep on the email and re-read in the morning. The fourth and final lesson, have someone read the email before sending. Well, I did not follow any of those four lessons. My comments were very pointed and written in red after every section in the minutes. Instead of typing an email with my points listed, I decided the best option was to type my comments on what was in the minutes at those sections. That way, the recipients would know exactly the context in which the comments were made and hopefully understand the direction that was given. One section apparently got everyone's attention.

The minutes stated that there were three possible solutions and that the third party engineer, the public works director and the contractor could not decide on the best solution. In other words, we had three potential solutions and three people that could not come together on a solution. This one set me off and my comments stated the following, "The direction was given at the prior PAR meeting to have solution and now we are month out from that meeting without any solution. We have three possible solutions and three people that can't decide what will work. All I see here is a three-ring circus without a decision being made. An agreed upon solution needs to be presented at the next PAR meeting and it had better go through the proper channels to ensure it is right". Needless to say, that got everyone's attention. This one could have been handled by sending an email directly to the public works director and the third party engineer with a copy to the city administrator. That was probably the correct action. There are times when a tone needs to be set and this was definitely one of those moments.

In conversation with John, the third party engineer, he stated that the email got everyone's attention at his office. They printed the email and took it to the contractor where it started a rather healthy discussion on potential solutions. The next PAR meeting was so much different in direction. By the way, we had a solution the week after my email and the construction commenced on boring under James River Freeway after the solution was accepted at the next PAR meeting. Sometimes a little global chewing goes a long way.

Josh Morris

Many events help shape our lives, some for the better and some for the worse. My first year as mayor was a year of shaping in a variety of ways. Josh Morris was a young man elected to the council in Ward 1. We served together for two years. He was a great council member and one that took his service in a serious manner. He was raised in Republic, graduated high school there and settled down in Republic after graduating college and getting married. He had two very young children when he was on the council and was always very attentive to their needs.

Josh had a knack for city government. Some people can serve all their lives and not fully understand the mechanism of government. Josh was a quick study and understood the role of council as it pertained to the growth of the city. He had a vision for what he thought Republic should be and potentially could be in the future. His opinions were well conceived, thorough and delivered with a force that was not overwhelming to the recipient, but allowed them to know he stood unabashedly behind his thoughts. Next to me, he was the youngest on the council by several years. Josh may have been the youngest council member, but Josh displayed a demeanor of maturity that was equaled by his knowledge on the agenda topics.

Josh and I did not know each other before we were on council together, but we became fast friends, especially during the times when we disagreed. Politics does not have to be personal, even though most people cannot talk about politics without making it personal. Josh and I may have disagreed on an occasion, such as the old fire truck, but it was never personal. We thought alike on the majority of topics and were not very far apart on the topics in which we were not in agreement. This allowed us to understand the thought process of the other when discussing a point on the council. The one thing that always impressed me about Josh was the fact that he had an open mind. Yes, he had strong opinions, but he also had an open mind when it came to the views of others. He was confident enough in himself to be able to change his opinion if he believed the other opinion was a valid one.

Life takes turns on all of us and it took one for Josh. Josh was married with two little children at home. Josh's dad was a barber in Republic and the pastor of the local United Pentecostal church. Josh and his wife grew up in the church. His wife stayed at home for the most part until she wanted to get job, which she did. This led to some independence and eventually discussion of divorce. They tried working out their marital issues for several months, but it was not meant to be at that point. Josh and his wife got a divorce. With two little children at home and shared custody, time spent with the kids was precious and thus ended Josh's council time. Josh's parent's and older sister Rachel lived close. They were able to help Josh with the children, but Josh chose time with his children instead of time with the council. Josh did not want to stop serving the city but did not have the time to devote to the council. We did have an opening on the planning and zoning commission. P&Z would not take up the amount of time that serving on the Council did and kept Josh involved in the community, therefore he was appointed to the planning and zoning commission.

Over the course of the next year, Josh and I stayed in touch. He would stop by the house every now and then to say hello with the kids after an ice cream run or a fresh air drive in the evening. I was elected Mayor in April 2008 and Josh would always joke with me about running against me at the next election. Josh did aspire to become the mayor and he would have made an excellent one! One of those evenings that Josh stopped by was Friday, August 1, 2008. Josh pulled up in the van with the kids after an ice cream run. It was a beautiful August evening and not as hot as it usually is that time of year. We talked with the kids for a while then stepped away to have a quick discussion on how the custody was going with the kids along with how they were managing it. Josh stated that the kids were doing fine and that he was delivering them to his ex-wife on Sunday afternoon, since he had them that weekend.

On Sunday, August 3, 2008, the house phone rang with a number that I did not recognize. As I was right in the middle of something, I did not pick up immediately but finished what I was doing. Just as I went to pick it up, it stopped ringing, lucky for me since it turned out to be one of the local radio stations. Radio stations, television stations and the newspapers would call when they wanted my opinion or comments on a story. My cell phone rang immediately and the number that came up was that of our Police Chief, Mark Lowe. When I answered, Chief asked me if I was sitting down and told him yes. He asked me to come down to the Police station as soon as possible and then proceeded to tell what happened to Josh.

Josh delivered the children to their mother on that Sunday afternoon. The summer heat had returned to southwest Missouri that day with temperatures in the upper 90's and humid. It was hot outside just sitting in the shade. Josh had agreed to meet his ex-wife and mother of his two children in one of the parks in Republic. The park was located in between two elementary schools. At that time, there was a gravel parking lot where the two rest rooms were located and it was centrally located in the park. Josh pulled in and parked his van awaiting his ex-wife keeping the air conditioning running to keep the kids cool. She pulled in next to him on his driver's side. She got out of the vehicle, as did Josh, so they could have any discussion outside the vehicles away from the kids. She came around her vehicle and a heated discussion began in between the vehicles over custody again. By this time, the kids were looking out the window at their parents talking. The discussion continued for a few minutes, when she pulled out a 9mm pistol and shot Josh in the head. The children were in the van and witnessed the entire episode. She called 911 in hysterics stating, "Please help me, please help me!"

Josh was taken to the nearest hospital in Springfield, 8 miles away, where he died of a single gunshot to the head and massive brain trauma. The ex-wife was put in custody and charged with murder. I arrived at the Police station that Sunday afternoon and received a briefing from the Chief. Josh's parents were there along with his sister and her family. The two children were in a room designed for children and they were being occupied with toys and other items while things were being sorted. There was not much that can be said in that moment with his family and I really do not remember what was said, other than I am so sorry.

The press showed up at the police station not long after the 911 call along with the city administrator Jim Krischke. The press heard the 911 call and had called my house. It was divine intervention that I did not pick up that call. It was devastating enough to hear what happened from the Police Chief but to hear it on a phone call from the press would have been so much worse. At the police station, we kept the family in the back and the press outside as Chief, Jim and I discussed what was going to be said. We briefly discussed with the family what was going to be said, what was not going to be said and wanted them to be aware that we were going to stick to the script until the investigation was over, which would take some time. Chief Lowe addressed the media and answered all their questions. There are times that the mayor needs to be heard and other times when the mayor does not need to be heard. This was not my time to be heard, it was the Police Chief's time to be heard.

As investigations go, this one went rather quickly. His ex-wife had legally purchased the 9mm Taurus handgun at Bass Pro Shops the day before on Saturday, August 2nd. On the way to jail on that Sunday, she was being interviewed by a Republic detective and stated that, "I shot him." There were many other details of the investigation and all of it pointed at the premeditation of the ex-wife.

As trials go, this one did not go quickly. The ex-wife had a history of mental issues and that created a long process to establish whether she could stand trial. At her initial sentencing, she was admitted to a mental hospital and labeled as unfit to stand trial. Several years passed and the trial was put on hold numerous times. On September 6, 2011, she entered an Alford plea, thus, avoiding a trial. An Alford plea means that she did not admit guilt but acknowledges that the evidence is sufficient to allow a judge to make a finding of guilt. In February, 2012, she was sentenced to 20 years in prison.

Josh's life was taken from him, but the worst part is that his children will now grow older without a loving dad, father, friend and confidant. Justice will never be complete when it involves a homicide, regardless of the sentence.

Brian C. Buckner

Jim Huntsinger

J im Huntsinger saw things a certain way and believed his way was the best way. Mr. Huntsinger was retired military, worked in the work world and even taught school for a while. He was a long serving council member and had been a part of the council when the city of Republic went through two very important issues in the late 1990's. The first issue was the possible relocation of the sewer treatment plant. The second issue was the battle with the ACLU on the ichthys on the Republic flag. An ichthys is a fish symbol created by two arches intersecting at one point and joining at another point.

The sewer issue was a hotly contested discussion where four votes went to the citizens for approval over the course of three years. In 1995, the sewage treatment plant exceeded its capacity and an agreement calling for an expansion was executed by the Missouri State Attorney General's office and the Missouri Department of Natural Resources. Basically, the city of Republic pumps its sewage uphill and the treatment plant had exceeded the capacity for which it was certified. Something had to be done to avoid the fines by the state. The sewer plant was located in the northwest part of town, which also is one of the higher points in the area. The proposed sewer plant would be a down flow type of system. As it was, the sewage flowed mostly down to a central location in the southeast part of town utilizing gravity to move it. At that point, the sewage was pumped back up hill to the sewer treatment plant on the northwest part of town utilizing large electric pumps to move the sewage. The pumps were arranged along the way to move the sewage. Other pumps in the community moved sewage as well, but the main pumps moved the sewage up hill. At the bottom where the sewage started its trek back up hill, the sewage was pumped 4.5 miles in the lines to the treatment plant. 42% of all sewage in Republic made this trek. At a few points in the city the sewage traveled 22 miles to make it to the treatment plant. At a town hall meeting during my second mayoral term, the 22-mile fact was shown on a map that had lines drawn out 22 miles from Republic showing the distance some of the sewage traveled.

At the time, Republic had 9 pump stations situated throughout the community. For a population of around 7,000 in 1996, that was a bunch of pump stations. In contrast, a large city in Nebraska had a total of 11 pump stations for a population of almost 400,000 in 1996. There was a need to relocate the sewage treatment plant. The costs were increasing by the year with the uphill pumping. Submersible sewage pumps are large and expensive. By switching to a down flow system, the city could save money on the pumps themselves over their life cycle and increase the capacity of the plant, which was needed.

In researching this issue for a new sewage plant, the city concluded that the best location would be in the southeast portion of the community in an area with few houses. It was also concluded that the plant could be built with extra capacity to accommodate the future growth that would be occurring in Republic. Meetings were held with the community and the council seemed divided at the time. Mr. Huntsinger was a strong supporter of the plant not being relocated. This stance was not a very popular one with the city staff and everyone that knew something had to be done to avoid fines from the state of Missouri. Mr. Huntsinger stood by his views unwavering in the face of criticism. The council decided to send the vote to the people, since it would require the city issuing bonds to pay for the new plant and that required a vote of the people. The first election occurred in November, 1996, with a location of the Shuyler Creek basin for the location and 10.6 million dollars in proposed bonds to fund the project. The proposal was defeated.

This did not solve the issue with the overcapacity, the high cost and the fact that the state was ready to fine Republic for exceeding its capacity. The second proposal was to move the proposed treatment plant further downstream to a location that was directly south of the Wilson Creek National Battlefield. This proposal had 11.6 million in bonds for the funding. The election for the new site and the increased funding took place in April, 1997. It was also defeated.

The third proposal had the new plant back at the original Shuyler Creek basin location and 11.6 million in bonds for funding this time. The city held meetings with the citizens that contained a much more detailed view of the project. The thought was that with more education on the project the voters would approve the project. The election for the third proposal took place in August, 1997. It was also defeated.

The city was clearly in a situation that did not have a good ending in sight. A fourth proposal was presented to the citizens that targeted expansion of the current facility and it was funded by 14.3 million in bonds. The proposal was for expansion only not allowing for any upgrades to the current system other than expansion. It would have been less expensive to build a new treatment facility than expand the current one by 3.7 million dollars. This proposal passed.

Mr. Huntsinger made a name for himself on this issue. Some say it was a bad name while others a good one. One thing was clear. If people did not believe Mr. Huntsinger stood by his opinions, then the next issue would completely get their attention. The Republic logo at the time was a circle with four quadrants inside that was adopted by council in 1991 under Mayor Gerry Poole. Mayor Poole had some local high school students come up with designs that she brought to the council for a vote. On the logo, the upper left quadrant had a blue background with a white picture of the state of Missouri. A yellow star was located in the state where Republic was located. In the upper right quadrant, there were two hands clasping on a red background. The hands signified the helping nature of the community. The bottom right quadrant had a green background with a silhouette of a family with a mother and father standing beside each other with the two kids in front of them. This obviously signified the family atmosphere of the community. The bottom left quadrant was a white background with an ichthys in black on it. The ichthys or ichthus is a Greek symbol which is an acronym basically translated at "Jesus Christ, God's son, Savior". This was representing the religious history of Republic. This is also where the city came into a situation with the American Civil Liberties Union or ACLU.

The ichthys symbol came under fire from a Republic resident who practiced Wicca and was a part of the Wiccan faith. She opposed the symbol on the grounds the symbol violated separation of church and state along with the fact that it endorsed the Christian faith. According to the lady, she started to receive hate mail after she wrote an editorial opposing the city seal which contained the ichthys. The ACLU became involved with a lawsuit filed in July, 1998. It demanded that the city remove the symbol from the city's logo and subsequently all the city owned items with the logo.

The community was behind the push to fight the lawsuit. A citizen formed a committee and they raised $35,000 for the defense of the impending lawsuit. The National Law Foundation represented the city pro bono against the ACLU lawsuit.

All of this was going on at the same time the city was embroiled in the sewer treatment plant issue. These two topics were in the news at every meeting and were headlining the print media and the television media (social media was not a relevant source of news at the time.) One of these topics would have been enough for a community, but Republic was dealing with both simultaneously and Mr. Huntsinger was on the not-so-popular side of both. He opposed the sewer plant relocation and now he opposed fighting the lawsuit with the ACLU. These were not popular opinions and Mr. Huntsinger was not afraid to voice his opinions. The city of Republic fought the lawsuit as much as possible with assistance and eventually the case went before a Federal judge.

In a summary judgment on July 9, 1999, Senior Judge Russell G. Clark of the Federal District Court for the Western District of Missouri wrote, "...when viewing the fish on Republic's flag, a reasonable observer would conclude that it is a Christian religious symbol. While the citizens of Republic may have intended that its seal send only a message of moral values or promote 'a universal symbol of religion,' an applaudable motive cannot save the city seal from a violation of the Establishment Clause. While the purpose of placing the fish on the city seal may not have been to endorse Christianity, the effect of the seal is to do so. The portrayal of the fish impermissibly excludes other religious beliefs or non-beliefs and--intended or not--depicts Christianity as the religion recognized and endorsed by the residents of Republic," Judge Clark added. "The Republic city seal pervasively invades the daily lives of non-Christians and sends a message that they are outsiders. The Constitution forbids such a result." Remember, this was in 1999.

Mr. Huntsinger was an ardent supporter of not pursuing the lawsuit. His stance came from a pragmatic standpoint the city just simply did not have the funding for a long drawn out lawsuit regardless of whether some of the legal representation would be without cost. The city lost the short lawsuit when the summary judgment was made. Mr. Huntsinger had solidified his place among many residents as they assumed he was one that would not support the city and did not want progress. Both assumptions on Mr. Huntsinger were not accurate. Mr. Huntsinger was in fact a Christian and attended a Southern Baptist church. A few years later, Mr. Huntsinger attended the church pastured by Mayor Collins. Mr. Huntsinger was a realist in the fact that he did not want to see the city spend taxpayer money on a lawsuit it was going to lose for all practical purposes. Emotions were involved on the sewer issue and certainly emotions ran high on the ichthys issue. When emotions run high on political issues, the personal attacks are soon to follow and Mr. Huntsinger endured those attacks. Not to say that some of that was not brought on himself, but character assassinations do not have any part in life. Mr. Huntsinger would later tell me that his stance on the sewer issue was not the correct one and if he had to do it all over, he would have supported the relocation of the sewer treatment plant. Conversely, Mr. Huntsinger would not change his opinion on the ichthys issue. He still believed it would have been a gross waste of taxpayer funds.

My first council meeting as a council member representing Ward 3 had me sitting in between two of the most senior and veteran council members. Garry Wilson sat on my left from Ward 2 and Mr. Huntsinger sat on my right from Ward 4. Mr. Huntsinger was very gracious in his approach to me letting me know what was being said and how each vote would be taken, whether it was a show of hands vote or a roll call vote. One of Mr. Huntsinger's first pieces of advice to me regarded information being presented in an executive session. As the information was being delivered from Mayor Collins, I was taking a few notes. Mr. Huntsinger leaned over to me and quietly told me to watch what was written in executive session. Note taking would have been fine, but since the subject matter had not yet become public knowledge, my notes should be disposed of directly after the meeting, kept in a safe place or not written at all. Note to self, do not take notes during executive session.

Over the years, Mr. Huntsinger and I became good friends and he was elected as the mayor pro tem four times during my years as mayor until the day he resigned from council. The mayor pro tem was elected every year by council. One thing that Mr. Huntsinger got himself into that would just cause me to shake my head was the coffee shop talk. Almost every morning, Mr. Huntsinger would have coffee and breakfast with a group of retired gentlemen at one of the local restaurants. During this discussion, inevitably city business would come up and they all looked to Mr. Huntsinger for his opinions. They enjoyed giving him their opinions. At times, it seemed that they hoped he would take their ideas back to city hall for implementation. Mr. Huntsinger would finish his coffee and breakfast with his usual stop by city hall on the way home to his wonderful wife Doris. While at city hall, Mr. Huntsinger would usually stop by Jim Krischke's office and let him know all the things that were discussed at the coffee shop. As most topics discussed, usually everyone concluded that something needed to be done about what was discussed.

Jim Krischke would call me with the latest topics that were discussed. Inevitably each topic needed to be addressed immediately by the City before it got out of hand. After attempting to address a few of these issues, it became apparent quickly that all the topics discussed did not need to be addressed. Much of the talk that goes on regarding city politics or city government is just talk. Unless a person is on the inside of the government and in the position where decisions are made, all of it is just talk and speculation. A few topics actually had validity, but I made the decision to not address the coffee shop topics directly, but create a solution before the topic was brought to the forefront of the city. This worked well on those topics that were valid and did come to the forefront. The city already had a solution or had investigated the situation with a recommendation in hand before the complaint was made. One additional decision that I made involved letting Jim Krischke filter the coffee shop topics for validity. Once he determined if any had validity, he would call me and present those to me for a final decision on any action that would be taken. It is my estimation that about 90% of topics that were brought forward never received any action. Out of the remaining 10% that did see action, less than half ever came before the city administration or council.

As the mayor pro tem, Mr. Huntsinger had access to the city administrator and would take advantage of it. Coffee shop talk would almost be a daily occurrence. Over time and after many discussions, Mr. Huntsinger began to see that the coffee shop talk was not productive and rarely valid. He did begin to filter the topics brought forward and the truly legitimate topics did require action or at least research into a solution. One day during my second mayoral term in early 2011, Mr. Huntsinger asked to see me at my office at city hall. This did not happen often, since he would call me on the phone with anything he wanted to say or discuss. I arrived at city hall and Mr. Huntsinger was already there. At this point in his life, Mr. Huntsinger's health was not the best. He carried oxygen with him and used a walker to maneuver from place to place. Mr. Huntsinger could walk, but his lungs did not have the capacity to sustain his 6'2" frame when it was moving.

Mr. Huntsinger sat down in the office and told me about his health issues. He felt that he was not a productive member of the council. I let Mr. Huntsinger know that he was still a valuable member of the council and he was still mayor pro tem. He felt that he needed to resign from council to concentrate on his health and that the council would be fine without him. It was my opinion that Mr. Huntsinger did not like using the walker and did not want his oxygen beside him at the council meetings, since his council chair was closest to the audience. I assured Mr. Huntsinger that he was a valuable member of the council and that he was definitely needed. He had history on many of the projects around the city and could relay the thought process of the decisions made on those projects. I talked Mr. Huntsinger into staying on the council.

About six months later, Mr. Huntsinger called again for a meeting in my office. I knew exactly what the conversation was going to be about and agreed to meet with him. Mr. Huntsinger wanted to resign from the council and he was not going to let me talk him out of it. I agreed to his request to resign and we worked out a timeframe to get a replacement to the council so the Ward would have a constant two representatives. Not that I had to agree to his resignation for him to resign, but I really wanted him to stay and would have attempted to talk him out of it again. I agreed to not try and talk him out of it. Mr. Huntsinger resigned gracefully from council after eleven and a half years serving the city. This did not include the few years in which he was not on the council, so it was not a consecutive eleven and a half years. After Mr. Hunstinger's retirement from the council, we kept in touch and would see each around Republic. Mr. Huntsinger would still attend some of the local functions and still have coffee almost every day with his coffee shop friends, including his best friend David. On Wednesday, February 27, 2013, Mr. Hunstinger had a medical condition that caused him to collapse on his way to his car after his coffee shop meeting. Mr. Huntsinger passed away later that morning.

Mr. Huntsinger was an integral part of Republic with his service and his undeniable stance on the two most controversial topics in the history of Republic. He was a good friend, confidant and excellent council member even when we did not agree on a topic. He always kept it professional with me. Mr. Jim Huntsinger was a controversial figure in the history of Republic politics, but he loved the community, was an outstanding council member, mayor pro tem and wonderful friend.

Side Story: History is long and memories are apparently longer. After I was elected mayor, Mr. Huntsinger was elected as the mayor pro tem in 2008. It surprised many people that the council would elect an older retired military man as the mayor pro tem to the newly elected younger mayor (I was 40 at the time of my first mayoral election win while Mr. Huntsinger was 76 at the time.) A few of the citizens in town questioned why I selected Mr. Huntsinger as the mayor pro tem. They questioned why a forward thinker like me would pick a person that prohibited growth and was against religion in the community, according to them. That line of thinking was at least 10 years old, but some of the good citizens of Republic never forgot the issues that encompassed Mr. Huntsinger's stance on topics. This was also the perfect opening to explain how the mayor pro tem was selected by the entire Council and how the council process actually worked. It also gave me an opening to explain that Mr. Huntsinger was as forward thinking as I was and that he was one of the most supportive of any of the council members at the time. The perception of Mr. Huntsinger seemed to change after that point and he continued to enhance his reputation as one of the most respected voices in the community on and off the council.

How a Municipal Government Operates

The city of Republic had a few changes in its operations beginning in 1992. The original city council was called the board of Alderman. The board of Alderman was changed to city council starting with the adoption of the city charter in 2007. For ease of recounting my service to the city, I use the term "council" although I served 2005-2007 as a board member of the alderman form of government.) This change occurred with adopting the charter. I have a plaque that states "Brian C. Buckner Ward 3 Alderman" and one that has it listed as "Council Member".

The first city administrator was Dean Thompson in 1994-2007. He was also an alderman before taking on the city administrator position. The second city administrator was Jim Krischke from 2007-2016. The third city administrator was David Cameron hired in 2016 and as of this writing is still the city administrator. The city was a fourth class city until the home rule charter of 2007.

The city council is divided into four Wards with two citizens elected out of each ward for representation. Each person elected represented around 2,100 citizens in a community of 17,000. The ward map has changed over the years due to the growth of the city and the city has gone to great links to ensure there was not any type of gerrymandering during the changes. Each ward has approximately the same number of citizens represented or as close as it can get.

The actual council has a representative from each ward sitting across from the other ward representative. It goes in order on each side with a member of each ward represented. In addition, each council seat and the mayor position were two year terms at that time. Looking at one side of the council table there are four representatives. Two of those representatives will be up for election one year, while the other two will be up for the election the following year. This was designed so that each side of the table has the possibility of only two council members changing at one election. Four total members of council could possibly be changed at one election from the entire council. Two of those will sit on one side of the table and the other two will sit at on the other side of the table.

At council meetings, the city of Republic had two types of voting – roll call vote and a general vote or show of hands vote. Different types of legislation directed the type of vote used. The city had forms for legislation, ordinances and resolutions. All ordinances required two readings and a roll call vote at the end of the second reading. Resolutions were read, discussed and voted on using a general vote or show of hands vote at the same meeting. There are distinct differences in voting, but most casual observers would not catch the difference. Some definitions below may help.

Ordinances: Laws that set a zoning or a new law or some type of official long term legal action. Budget amendments were also part of this process. Ordinances required two readings. In other words, at one meeting the council would have the ordinance read once and discussion would take place from the council and staff. No final vote would be taken. At the next meeting, the council would have a second reading with another discussion and then a roll call vote. A roll call vote was an individual vote stated out loud when the council

93

members name was called. This was done for a variety of reasons, but in essence it was to ensure that there would not be any mistakes on how a council member voted.

Resolutions: These were more along the line of approval items for council. Scrivener errors, corrections, purchases, contract awards and other types of business would be by resolutions. A Scrivener error was basically a typographical error on a legal document that the council was reviewing. If the city needed a repair of a sewer pump or purchase a new vehicle, the resolution would be the avenue in which it was presented to council. Resolutions required a general vote or show of hands vote. It was the type of vote where everyone would vote at the same time with an "Aye" or "No" or "Abstention". There were times during a resolution vote that either a council member didn't vote or looked like they didn't vote or it didn't sound like all the council members voted. At this point, I would tell the council that we were going to vote again and that all members needed to vote. The council members knew it was coming when the voices didn't sound like all of them. The council members would know if they heard me say, "Let's try that again, all in favor say aye...." If the vote seemed to be a tie, then I would ask the council for a show of hands for either "Aye", "No" or "Abstention". This would be a more accurate count of the "Aye's", "No's" and "Abstentions".

We followed Robert's Rule of Order during council meetings under my tenure and during my time on council with Mayor Collins unless a specific ordinance, resolution or state law superseded Robert's Rules. There was a certain way that a first read of an ordinance had to be done and a certain way a second read had to be done. There seemed to be a lot of votes being taken by the council and to the average person, it seemed like the council was "rubber stamping" everything. It was difficult to see from the outside, but once understood, it was the right way to handle the council proceedings.

For example, we have the first reading of ordinance "Bill #05-17". It is an ordinance that would require two readings. The first reading would require a motion, a second, a vote to read, a reading of the bill, discussion and then move on to the next topic. Here is how this ordinance would be handled in abbreviations: ***M, 2ⁿᵈ, V, R, Discuss, MO***.

> Mayor to the council: "I would like to have a motion to have the first reading of Bill #05-17". (Some would add "...by title only please.") This is just to have the motion be approved to be read in front of Council.
>
> A council member: "I make that motion". M (Motion)
>
> Mayor: "Do I have a second on that motion?"
>
> A council member: "I second that motion." 2nd (Second)
>
> Mayor: "All in favor of the motion to have the first reading of Bill #05-17, say 'Aye'".
>
> The council: "Aye" (It was a general vote at this time). V (Vote)
>
> Mayor: "All opposed say 'No'".
>
> The council: "No" – if there were any. The first reading was just to get the bill in front of council and usually a "no" vote was not necessary unless someone did not want to discuss the bill.
>
> Mayor: "Any abstentions?"
>
> The council: Anyone wishing to abstain from this vote would signify with "I abstain". This rarely happened.

City Clerk: The city clerk would read the
official ordinance. R (Read)
The staff: I would ask the staff member to give
an overview and the staff member would give
an overview without their opinion.
The council: The council would ask questions
at this point. Discuss
After the discussion the council would move on
to the next topic. MO (Move On)

To the casual observer, a vote was taken on the topic,
however it was only to read the ordinance, not to
approve or disapprove it. Once the City Clerk read it,
the mayor would instruct the staff member to give the
council an overview. The staff member presenting the
bill would give an overview without any prejudice
whatsoever. It was not staff's job to tell the council how
to vote nor was it their job to lead council a certain way.
They were to present, be neutral, but there were
occasions when a recommendation from staff was
required. Once the overview was finished, the council
could ask questions regarding anything that pertained
to the bill. If a question was asked that was not part of
the general discussion of that bill, the question and or
comment would not be recorded and the mayor or
attorney would get the discussion back on track.

After the discussion and questions, the mayor would
move to the next item on the agenda. It was a first
reading without any final vote being taken. The final
vote would be taken at the second reading which was
usually at the next meeting unless it was tabled. The
abbreviation notation of *M, 2ⁿᵈ, V, R, Discuss, MO*
was always added by me to the top of each first reading
on my agenda documentation. This was done in pen
and then compared with what was written by the
attorney to ensure we both had the same process and

checked off each point in the process. Even though we had been through the same process for years, we would make the same notations and compare before every meeting and check as we went through every meeting. It was our way to ensure we were on the same page regarding the process. After each point in the notation was completed, the attorney would scratch through that point. Once the motion was made, the attorney would scratch the "M" on the notations on the bill. This was done to ensure that we stayed on track. The city administrator also had a role in keeping notes from the meeting. The city administrator would always have a cross drawn with four quadrants. In the upper left quadrant was the letter "M". In the upper right was the number "2". In the bottom left quadrant the city administrator would enter the name of the council member that made the "Motion" or "M". In the bottom right quadrant, the city administrator would add the name of the council member that seconded or "2" the motion. The city clerk was in charge of keeping track of all the information as it transpired around the council table. Sometimes our meetings would move rather quickly at times and extra notes were always useful. Other times the discussion could go long and the notations would allow us to know exactly where we were in the process.

Using the same ordinance, Bill #05-17, the second reading would be at the next meeting. This process was a little bit more complicated. It required a motion, a second, vote to read, a reading of the bill, a vote to approve the bill, a second, discussion and a roll call vote. In abbreviated notation form: ***M, 2, V, R, M, 2, Discuss, RC.*** This portion required that we get approval to have the second reading which required a vote. It then required us to have a motion and second to have final passage. This gave us the ability to pass it, table it or defeat it.

> Mayor to the council: "I would like to have a motion to have the second reading of Bill #05-17". (Some would add "...by title only please.")
>
> A council member: "I make that motion". M (Motion)
>
> Mayor: "Do I have a second on that motion?"
>
> A council member: "I second that motion." 2nd (Second)
>
> Mayor: "All in favor of the motion to have the second reading of Bill #05-17, say 'Aye'".
>
> The council: "Aye" (It was a general vote at this time). V (Vote)
>
> Mayor: "All opposed say 'No'".
>
> The council: "No" – if there were any.
>
> Mayor: "Any abstentions?"
>
> The council: Anyone wishing to abstain from this vote would signify with "I abstain".
>
> City Clerk: The city clerk would read the official ordinance. R (Read)
>
> Mayor to the council: "I would like to have a motion to have the final passage of Bill #05-17".
>
> A council member: "I make that motion". M (Motion)
>
> Mayor: "Do I have a second on that motion?"
>
> A council member: "I second that motion." 2nd (Second)
>
> The staff: The staff would give an overview of the bill.
>
> The council: The council would ask questions and have discussion at this point. Discuss

Once discussion ended, a roll call vote would be taken. RC

The process was very important since many meetings seem to get off track quickly on discussing an item. Additionally, the second read looked like more voting without discussion, but the process is fairly simple. Basically, the council had to approve the second reading of the bill. The bill then had to be read after approval. A motion to pass the bill was made next. An overview of staff was given and the council discussed the information. At the end, a roll call vote was taken. A roll call vote entailed the city clerk asking each member of the council how they vote on the bill. Aye, No or Abstain. Roll Call votes are taken individually and out loud.

A resolution was a different type of product that is brought before council. As the definition stated previously, a variety of topics could be covered with resolutions. The format for a resolution was slightly different than an ordinance. Resolutions only took one reading with a vote. The resolution was read, a motion made to approve, a second, discussion and a vote. Resolution notations were as follows: ***R, M, 2, D, V.***

The mayor would read the resolution. In some municipalities the city clerk reads the resolution, but in Republic the mayor read the resolutions.

Mayor: "Resolution #07-17. A resolution of the city council of Republic, Missouri authorizing the city administrator to enter into negotiations with ....for a third party IT contract. ***R***

Mayor to the council: "I would like to have a motion to approve Bill #07-17".

A council member: "Motion" ***M***

Mayor: "Do I have a second on that motion?"

99

A council member: "Second" **2**

Staff: The staff would give an overview of the resolution.

Council: Discussion would take place on the resolution. **D**

Mayor: After discussion, the mayor would say, "All in favor, say 'Aye'. Opposed, say 'No'. Any abstentions?" **V**

The process of an ordinance and a resolution are very similar yet distinct in their approach to what is being done by the council. An ordinance could fail immediately if the vote failed on having the reading, whether it was the first or second reading. If that happened, the ordinance would be dead for 90 days in Republic during my tenure. Other municipalities may have a different time frame or not any timeframe for an ordinance to return to the agenda. On a resolution, it could fail after the reading if the council did not approve the reading. It would also be dead for 90 days.

Those are the basics of operation for the city council of Republic. Inside of that framework, there were a few things that could occur which could change the course of the agenda item. A few of those things are: call for the question, table to a future date, table indefinitely, emergency second read and motions to amend. These are just a few items that can be done while discussing an agenda item.

Call for the question: This was done by a council member during the discussion (**D**) phase in the process. If the discussion was running long or at a point where nothing was really getting accomplished, a council member could "Call for the question". This ended all discussion and a vote would be taken. The vote was either a general vote or a roll call vote, depending on the type of the agenda item. Council members would rarely use this tactic to limit discussion on an item, but it was a tool in the council discussion tool box in case. This was used on me as a council member when we discussed the old fire truck. I lost that vote and immediately thought to myself, "When you lose, don't lose the lesson." Lesson learned. I used this to close the discussion during the meeting where the mayor had a council member removed. We had reviewed that information so much and after that incident, we needed to move on with the other agenda items. It worked effectively.

Table to a future date: If an item needed further answers for council or additional information was required or a change had occurred on the agenda item, the council could table the item to a future date. The date was required if the council wanted to finish their discussion of the item. Once the item was back on the agenda on the date specified, the council would take up the discussion where it left off. I usually asked staff for an overview, which was not required. We wanted everyone to be back on the same page before discussion commenced. Table to a future date did happen, just not very often.   The most common use when clarification was needed for the council. It could happen for a variety of other reasons, which could include the desire to have a full council present to vote in case a majority was not present. On any tabled item, a motion had to be given to remove the item from the table and a vote passed before a tabled item could be discussed.

Table indefinitely: This was essentially a quick way to kill the agenda item. There were circumstances that would require an agenda item to be killed and not voted on, but those times were few. An example would be an ordinance that would change a zoning classification on a piece of property. The ordinance would have a first read and then go to the second, but in between the first and second read, the applicant no longer wanted to pursue that zoning classification. Instead of voting down the ordinance to kill it, the council could make a motion to table indefinitely. If a second was given and the vote passed, the ordinance was tabled indefinitely without a date for a vote thereby effectively killing it. In my 8 years as mayor and 3 years as a council member, I can only remember about 2 or 3 that were tabled indefinitely. All were at the request of the applicant and had nothing to do with how the council viewed the item. A motion to table indefinitely only required a simple majority. In our situation, 5 members out of 8 would need to vote to table indefinitely. If there were less than a full council of 8 members present to vote and enough to make a majority of 5 members present, a simple majority of those present could table the item. If 6 or 7 council members were present, then 4 would be the majority. If 5 members were present, then 3 members could table the item indefinitely. Not a widely used tactic to kill an agenda item. It was used properly by our council in situations that required it to be utilized and was never at the request of a council member to limit or eliminate discussion.

Emergency Second Read: Ordinances required two separate readings at two different meetings. The first read would take place at one meeting and the second could take place at either the next meeting or a meeting at a later date. There were times when an emergency second reading was required the same night as the first reading. After becoming mayor, one of my directions to staff was to limit emergency second reads to necessity only. This was to ensure the staff had fully completed their work in a timely manner. What we did not want to see in front of council was an emergency second read due to a staff member not getting the work completed that was required to hit a deadline or attempting to get an ordinance in place before something would be affected. That policy was given to the city administrator by me the first week in office and it virtually eliminated emergency second readings. We did have one emergency read at the same time every year. In Missouri, the state sets the levy for the city and gives the municipalities until the end of August to vote and approve the new levy. Our council meetings, at the time, were held on the second and fourth Monday's of each month. The state would always send us our levy after the first meeting in August. Due to this timing, the first reading would take place at our second meeting in August which necessitated an emergency second reading at the same meeting in order to hit the state deadline of passage by the end of August. It wasn't ideal, but in all likelihood, the council was not going to vote down the state levy. We were going to receive it regardless, but the state required a vote, so we voted.

Motions to Amend: Motions to amend are the most commonly used council tactics and the most needed. Amendments could take the form of addition, change or subtraction of contents. Agenda items were not perfect at times and there were times that something would need to be modified to an agenda item that the council thought was needed. Other times, an amendment was needed to award a bid for a purchase, which was the most common use of motions to amend. For example, an agenda item was to award the bid for the purchase or contract of raw materials used in road construction and other city needs. The agenda item contained all the raw materials and each company that made a bid on those items. Rock, chat, sand, gravel (of different sizes) and a few other items would be on the bid specification sheet or spec sheet.

Each company would submit their bid in sealed envelope form. A date was specified for the bid opening and the bids were all opened at once. Once all the bids were opened, they became public knowledge and added to the agenda item. At the next Council meeting, the agenda item contained all the spec items with the companies listed along with their bid price. The staff would point out the lowest bidder under each raw material and the Council could view all the prices submitted. At this point, the agenda item was to award the bid of raw materials, it did not contain a specific company that would be awarded the bid – it was up to council to make the decision on which company received the award and for which raw material. The staff could recommend the lowest bidder and did so the majority of time. At this point, the council would ask the staff member for their recommendation and the staff member would usually recommend the lowest bidder. Once council was satisfied that the companies were receiving the correct bids, a motion would be made to add the set of companies with their bid award to the agenda item. This would make the agenda item complete and it could then be further discussed or voted on at that point. A quick side note: the council usually awarded to the lowest bidder, but that was not always the case. There could be times when the council or the staff member had issues in the past with the lowest bidder and the award would go to another bidder. There had to be concrete evidence or a legitimate reason for not awarding to the lowest bidder, but it did happen occasionally. For example, a bid on a new backhoe came down to the purchase price on our old backhoe from the bidding companies. Each company met the all the bid specs on the new backhoe and the prices were within a few dollars of each other. The difference in bid came down to the purchase price of our current backhoe that we were replacing. A $200 higher bid price on the new one could easily be offset by a purchase price on the old one that was $4,000 higher than the low bidder on the new backhoe. That is actually a $3,800 savings off the lowest bidder for the new backhoe. So, before saying that the council or any municipal government always needs to take the lowest bidder, look deeply into the entire bid process and check the bid spec sheet. The lowest bid is not always the low bid.

Companies would use a variety of ways to get the lowest bid. If the bid was to be considered, it had to meet all the bid specs. In regards to the raw materials listed above, some companies would go low on the cost of one set of bid specs while going high on a few others. The dollars may end up being the same as the other companies, but on one specific item, they may be much lower which could be enticing to a council if they were only looking at one item. Asphalt companies seem to do this quite often and it usually involved transportation costs or the actual asphalt or concrete cost itself. At one council meeting we were approving a bid for all the landscaping work on an amphitheater project. It encompassed all the work including planting, moving ground, materials, labor, etc. The lowest bidder had one line item which was extremely high compared to the others, but this companies overall bid was the lowest by far. Unlike the vote for raw materials where the council could award the bid on separate items by separate companies, the bid for the landscaping was for the entire project. One company, one project. A council member questioned the bid based on the extreme high cost of one particular item. I remember it as $1,000 for landscaping plants or something to that effect. Since the bid was the lowest, the contractor chose to make up some of his difference in price by charging an exorbitant amount for landscaping plants, but the overall bid was still the lowest by far. The question by the council was answered take the entire bid or none of the bid. This type of bid spec manipulation did take place and does so quite often in any type of bid atmosphere.

Red Tape, Process and Zoning

Many facets to government require interaction with the citizens. In a smaller municipal government setting, the city has more local interaction with the citizens which can be positive or negative at times. The basic goal of a city is to create a structure in which citizens can live in a nice community with laws in place to keep the peace. Within that community, there will be times when disagreements occur or things need to change in order for a city to remain viable for the future. It is disagreements in operation or direction that seem to cause the most issues within a community. What type of building is constructed or what zoning classification a property is going to be can generate immense and intense discussion among citizens. Usually, the city government is at the epicenter of the discussion either by choice or by code. The city may have chosen to do something that does not meet with favor for the majority of the community or the city has enforced a code that has garnered attention and not well received. In either case, public outcry can be strong and emotional. There are many reasons that government does not do a good job with the community interaction. Some the reasons are legitimate and some are applied by the citizens due to a variety of factors.

Red Tape and Emotions. If anything, government is known for its red tape or processes or both. How many people get frustrated going to the department of motor vehicles? This could be just to license a vehicle or renew a license only to find out that they have to go to another area or fill out another form before moving on to the next process. The government process is rather daunting in some aspects, but the internet has made it easier to navigate the government process or red tape. For those that want to have that face-to-face experience, government is likely to give a lot of face-to-face experience over the course of the interaction, much of it not necessarily wanted. Everyone likes to deal with one person and not be passed from person to person to accomplish their goal, but that is actually sometimes necessary. Lack of red tape knowledge or government process understanding is what causes the strong emotions in citizens. The emotions get higher and higher with every process that doesn't accomplish the citizen's goal, therefore red tape and process breed emotions and subsequently cause ill will toward the government itself.

One way to help alleviate the red tape or reduce the process is to have employees that explain how the process works and assist citizens in getting to the right person to start the process. We would often have people call the public works department to start the process for a building permit. At the city of Republic at that time, the building permitting process starts and concludes in the planning department. Instead of the city employee telling the person inquiring that it is not their job or that permits are not handled there, the employee would explain the first step in the process is to get them to the planning department. The employee would give them the name of the individual they needed to talk to and transfer them to that person if they wished. It may sound simple to just transfer a call or direct them to the correct building, but a person would be surprised how often someone would have to drag out the information from the employee to get where they needed to go. It was up to our employees to reduce the red tape as much as possible by assisting the person in getting in contact with the individual that can assist them. If it was a complaint, the same process applied. The employee may listen to the entire complaint before letting them know the person that could assist with their issue. Yes, the employee may have endured a complaint unnecessarily, but the end result is to solve the issue of the citizen.

An old Yugoslav proverb stated, "Complain to the one that can help you." It was up to the city employee to ensure the complainant talked to the right person. Once the complainant had the person that could assist, it was the employee's responsibility to listen to the complaint. With that said, our city employees did not have to listen to personal attacks or threats and that would automatically escalate the issue to the city leadership, ultimately stopping with me. Whoever said the customer is always right was probably a customer that had never worked in government or business. The citizen is not always right and the government is not always right. Usually, most of the complaints in government deal with something that a citizen doesn't like happening in their neighborhood or around their business. Those are opportunities to solve problems, which is one philosophy of mine. Governments need to concentrate on solving problems before them and be proactive in addressing potential future issues.

In business and government, listening to one side without fully understanding the other side is common practice and not a good common practice. Some leaders, managers and entrepreneurs will listen to one person and agree with them. Then, they will listen to the other side and agree with them as well. This type of leadership/management style causes discourse and mistrust throughout the organization. Either the leader/manager does not have enough confidence in their answer or does not want to delve into the issue at that particular time. To get out of the situation, they agree with both sides so they can move on. The recipients believe their issues are resolved, when in actuality it is not resolved. When the recipients find out their issues are not resolved, the emotion is greater than it was the first time.

The majority of complaints are what I called persuasion complaints. The person was attempting to persuade the city to make a decision on a particular issue in their favor. What I learned over the years in government is that there are two sides to every story regardless of how well you know the person complaining. Many complainants will not tell the entire story, just their side of it. They want you to see their side only and that is their way of selling their solution. This occurs in every business. In sales, the product that is being presented can be presented in a variety of ways, from benefit to price to quality. How it compares to the competition or opportunity cost should be part of the selling discussion. The other side of selling is to understand the competition and address it upfront. In presenting their side to government, most citizens only present their side without looking at the other side of the situation. That would be similar to presenting a product without ever looking or understanding the competition. Sadly, elected officials and politicians can get caught up in one side without addressing the other side before making comments on the situation. (There is a difference between an elected official and a politician). They want to be responsive to the person in front of them, but are usually afraid of making them mad. There are times when the answer is "let me discuss this with the other person and I will get back with you." This delayed the answer and that allowed for a complete research of the issue before making a decision. It was the best path to follow in reviewing any type of complaint. Another answer that was often used by me, "We are going to have to agree to disagree". This was only used after some discussion, usually a lengthy discussion and it did let the person know that I was staying with my opinion and they could stay with their opinion.

Zoning issues usually generate discussion. Zoning changes are necessary in the city government. As communities expand, zoning changes will be required. The city has zoning classifications established with the types of businesses that can be in each zone. The zoning classifications usually entail some sort of retail class, manufacturing class, agriculture class and a myriad of residential classifications. Within each business class, the types of businesses are outlined and hopefully they are laid out in a clear way. For example, a recycling business wants to be a part of the community and is contemplating purchasing a piece of property that is zoned retail. The zoning classification for a recycling business is under the manufacturing zoning classification in Republic. The business has two choices, it can apply for a rezone of the property to allow for a recycling business or it can look for another piece of property that would be appropriate and is already zoned manufacturing. The request for a rezone would go through the planning and zoning board first before reaching city council. If the P&Z board refused the rezone, it would still come before the city council in Republic, per the charter, with the P&Z voting information. Usually, the city council did not override P&Z's recommendation. Bottom-line, P&Z made their recommendation, but the city council had the final vote on the rezone.

There could be another issue that might arise with this scenario. The issue of finding a piece of property that was zoned manufacturing, but the citizens in that area did not want that type of business located in their general area. This is where many governments get sideways with the citizens and businesses. The city council had clear direction in this scenario. The council could not deny based on the type of business that was part of the business classification that was approved for that area. If the property was properly zoned and the recycling business was part of that classification, in this case manufacturing, the city could not deny the business locating in the manufacturing zoning classification, unless there were major overriding issues that were involved. In this case, the city council can only deny a zoning request or plat based on three items, health, safety or welfare of the area. It would have to be some very serious issues for it to be denied.

Likewise, there are certain businesses that do not neatly fit into any type of zoning classification, such as, sexually oriented businesses or S.O.B.'s as Ron called them. These were usually adult night clubs or adult bars and their zoning classification had to be handled very carefully. Businesses such as these had to be classified in one class or another. That did not limit the city on the restrictions within this classification on the location. For example, the city could establish an ordinance that simply stated that an S.O.B. had to be further than 1,500 feet from a church or residential dwelling and no less than 2,000 feet from a school and city park. These types of restrictions allowed for this type of business, but it did allow the city to classify them within a zoning classification along with the restrictions. The stronger the restrictions, the harder it would be to locate in the community. The less restrictions the easier it would be to locate within the community. Every restriction and zoning classification had to be defensible in a court of law.

What a business or a house looks like can also be a tough proposition. Most communities like growth and new business. New business can build the building as they wish without too much consideration from the city government, but communities can protect themselves when it comes to how the business looks in certain areas. Cities can create corridors where there are requirements for any business in that area, such as historical district or retail corridor. The requirements could be fascia requirements or landscaping requirements or a multitude of different qualifiers for the business. At times, this lends itself to criticism from the business community due to the potential increased cost of the requirements, but it is a trend that works well with rapidly growing communities where consistency is needed across the broad spectrum of businesses.

On the housing side, cities do not necessarily have the same protection regarding the type of home built. There are usually different types of zoning classifications in residential ranging from apartments, duplex or zero lot line zoning to high density to medium density to low density. Within each classification, there are usually minimum lot sizes without any restrictions on how the dwelling looks, which is very subjective. This does not allow the city much control over the visual aspect, but there are certain types of projects that do allow the city a little control over the visual aspect of the dwelling. In Republic, we had a P.D.D., or Planned Development District. This was a piece of property that could contain multiple zoning classifications and different types of dwellings. For example, it could have retail zoning for business upfront, apartment zoning in the middle, duplex zoning next and high density zoning at the back of the property. In this case, the housing portion of P.D.D. could be presented to council with a visual aspect of how the apartments and duplexes might look. This is where a council could make a crucial mistake. First, the developer of the P.D.D. is not obligated to build to the visual specs shown to the council. The developer is only required to meet the zoning requirements of the P.D.D. Second, the council could attempt to enforce the developer to build what was shown to council which is where the mistake would take place. Council needs to know their role in the process and how it relates to the zoning classification along with the rules that apply. We had a P.D.D. that was a mix use of zero lot lines and two story duplexes. The city was shown some very nice artist renderings of the front of the proposed structures. When it came time to build, the structure fronts changed along with some of the basic structure sizes. The two story duplexes generated some controversy, since they were close to the back yards of an older subdivision that was zoned medium density. The second floor overlooked the back yard of the homes because of the second story was close to the property line. Everything was to code and fit the zoning classifications, but it was not what council thought they were getting in this P.D.D. The residents of the subdivision behind the P.D.D. were still not satisfied with the property behind them and council learned a valuable lesson the process.

The old Cox barn. In one of those situations where history and progress collide, Republic had a structure known as the Cox barn. The history of the barn is long and had a varied use over its life cycle. It was a very large barn with multiple stories and sat on a piece of city property with beautiful large trees around it. The location of the barn was at the end of a city park where three schools sat across from it. It was really a nice location and became city property after it was donated several years before. According to some, the barn was originally a dairy barn. It transitioned over the years to hold a variety of activities for the school and community including dances. The barn also served as the public library for a time as well. As other facilities were built, the barn lost most of its use, as well as becoming a hazard that didn't meet any of the fire and safety codes. Its use dwindled and eventually came to being used for storage by the city for years. The storage use even stopped as items were eventually moved to safer locations. It was still a sturdy barn, but liability insurance played a major role in the safety of the workers and a structure that did not meet safety requirements could easily be a target for a lawsuit if anything happened when working in the structure. Eventually, a discussion ensued on what to do with the barn. There were proposals from the historical society on raising funds to refurbish the barn and use it as a historical museum. The cost to make it safe made it out of reach for almost any community organization with limited funding. At the city, we discussed refurbishing it ourselves, but cost was the issue again. The decision was finally made to demolish the barn. An agreement was reached with the school district to remove the barn, leave the trees and the city would donate the property to the school district to build a park on the site. The barn was cleaned out and then leveled. A park was put in its place for the school district and the kids play on the site that held so many community events over the years. It was a fitting ending for a building that served the community well.

Everyone is Paid to Think

E veryone at the city had a role including elected officials. The elected official's role is to ensure the city is moving in the right direction and make decisions on the items presented. The mayor's role is guide the council during the meetings and work with the city administrator on ensuring the city is headed in the right direction. At council meetings in Republic's form of government, the council needs to make the decisions and the mayor should not give the mayor's opinion unless it is requested. This is where many councils and mayors get off the rails. The mayor may feel that they need to impart their wisdom on the council or try to guide them to a decision. This should not be the case. The mayor needs to understand the mayor's role in the government process. At one particular council meeting, the council voted to purchase a small building behind city hall to refurbish and lease the space to a small business. The building was not large and with a cost of $70,000, the only benefit was that it made the city property contiguous to the street behind city hall with a parking lot that would accommodate city employees. The property was purchased by the council during an executive session. After the meeting, we were celebrating a council member's birthday with cake and punch when a council member asked me what I thought of the building purchase. This is where things got interesting. Council members rarely asked my opinion and when my opinion was given, it seemed everyone listened. It reminded me of the old E.F. Hutton commercials, when E.F. Hutton speaks, everyone listens. In this case, I gave my opinion and it was short and succinct. I stated that I would have not voted to purchase the building. This caught most of the council members off guard, but one council member made a statement that still shocks me to this day. She stated, "Well, if I'd known that, I would not have voted for it." Therein lays the issue with the mayor giving the mayor's opinion all the time. That is why it is so important to let the council members do their job voting for the items and not try to persuade the council. One caveat on this type of arrangement. The council has to be objective in review and let the facts show through without prejudice. There were a variety of reasons to purchase the building and a variety of reasons not to purchase the building. Council thought it was a good idea and years later the council had to vote on whether to keep renting the building or whether to turn it back into a city office. The city chose to keep the building and return it to the city asset inventory after years of renting it to a café/pottery business.

Another philosophy is not to complain unless a solution is presented. This one seems so simple, but most do not have a solution to the issue for which they are complaining. The issue upsets them and they want to vent without completely thinking through the situation. Emotions are usually involved with this type of situation but that does not absolve the person from creating a solution. Everyone is paid to think regardless of their job or role. Complaining is easy, solutions are difficult. Case in point, the railroad track crossings to downtown Republic were extremely rough. So rough, that people would actually avoid the crossing and take an alternate route. Everyone complained, including everyone at the city and the public works director. The topic of the railroad tracks hit the PAR agenda. As usual, everyone complained how rough the crossing was. When I asked about why they hadn't been fixed, the public works director told us that those are property of the railroad and they would fix them when they wanted. All attendees elaborated and stated that the railroad was in Republic long before Republic existed and they were a bureaucracy that was worse than the federal government. The conversation wore on and everything that was stated explained why it could not be fixed by the city and how the railroad would get around to it when they wished. And so far, the railroad had not bothered with any of the four main crossings in Republic. It was easy to complain, but no one had a solution nor did anyone offer one. My first question was this one: "When was the last time we contacted the railroad about the main street crossing?" The answer was shocking. No one had contacted them, because they had not had any luck in years past, not necessarily on that intersection, but just contact in general. My next comment was very directional. Paraphrased, it stated, "Contact the railroad! Call until you get someone that knows something about our intersection. Relay the number of the complaints that we receive on that one intersection, but that we receive complaints on all four intersections. Ask them when they are going to repair the intersection and get back with us with an answer. The public works director called and talked with someone regarding our request.

At the next PAR meeting, the public works director relayed the answer of the railroad. The Main Street tracks in Republic were not on the agenda that year for repair. My instructions to the Public works director were very pointed. Call the railroad again, let them know we have discussed their answer and then offer to cost share the repair with them. Also communicate that we would like a start date for the repairs. The

Public works director stated that we did not budget for the repairs and that we did not have funds set aside for this type of repair. I reiterated my direction and said to not worry about any cost at this point. The Public works director was concerned with having to outlay any funds for the repairs, while I was concerned with repairing the tracks. That is concentrating on minutia versus vision. The Public works director returned at the next PAR meeting with an answer from the railroad. Their crews were not going to be in the area for the remainder of the year, so our area was not on the list of repairs. Additionally, they said that our crews were not covered on their insurance in case of an accident. Basically, the same answer as last time. My direction this time was more pointed. I instructed the Public works director to call the railroad again. This time tell them that the mayor, city administrator and attorney had approved our street department to repair the tracks and we would like a date that we could start the repairs. Communicate to them that since their crews were unavailable and we were not on their priority list, then we would take care of the repairs. We just need a date when the trains would not be in the sector. The public works director was reluctant to send this message and very apprehensive in his approach. I assured him that this would work out for the best and to make the call.

The next month when the public works director returned to the PAR meeting, he had a smile on his face. He relayed my message to the railroad and it was not received well. Apparently, plenty of conversation took place inside the railroad and agreement had been created. It is amazing what a little effort does in situations like this one. A couple of months later, we had an agreement with the railroad on repairing the Main Street crossing along with our assistance. We also had an agreement to repair the other three crossings within the city. When a group of individuals are all negative on an issue, take notice and try to figure out exactly what has been done. It may be that they are all correct. It could be they have the same mentality as some citizens. Government will not do what they are asking in this case improving the railroad crossings. Government with vision can find a way.

Solutions require creativity at times, especially financial solutions. While in a PAR meeting that the fire chief attended, he stated that the city needed a new fire truck. It was going to be expensive. Since most police and fire expenditures were from the general fund without any type of tax revenue, these types of purchases always seemed to be without solution. Funding would be an issue, but there was a need. The fire chief thought he had the solution in a cooperative agreement with other community fire departments in Springfield, Battlefield and Nixa. This would reduce the cost of the truck, since it was a cooperative purchase. In other words, it was a volume discount for those participating. The only issue, the discount was good, but not that good. The finance director at the time did not see any way to purchase the fire truck and complete financing was somewhat out of the question at that point. We asked the finance director and the fire chief to combine their thoughts and come up with a viable solution. The following week, the finance director stated they had a solution. Since there was not enough cash for an outright purchase and we did not want a large financed truck, the solution was unique. The city would purchase the chassis and finance the cab. The money for the chassis was affordable and the financing on the cab was low and could be paid off before the end of the service life of the vehicle. Where there is a will, there is a creative finance director to make it happen.

Side story: Don't end a sentence in a preposition. In a separate incident, the city was in need of a ladder truck for the fire department, not the truck in the above story where the chassis was purchased and the cab financed. This was a few years earlier when the department needed a ladder truck to help reduce the I.S.O. rating. With all the building going on in Republic, there were a few structures that were getting up there in height. A distribution center that had recently located in Republic was over 110 feet in height. The chief, who we called "Mr. eBay" for years due to his frugal deals and purchases, found a ladder truck. He found it on the internet and thought it was a great price. A new one at the time would cost well over a million dollars. Yes, it was used and below its real value, but he needed it with all the taller structures being constructed. My son was at his sixth grade football practice and I was there helping coach when my cell phone rang. It was the chief. When I answered, all he said was, "Guess what I am looking at?" It took every shred of decency to not tell him he just ended a sentence in a preposition; however, I was not going to fall into that trap. My answer was, "what are you looking at chief?" He responded with, "I am looking at the Pacific Ocean on one side, San Diego on the other and Tijuana, Mexico on the other. The view is wonderful." The fire truck he found was at a dealer in San Diego. He flew out there with another fire fighter to check out the truck. He had apparently taken a test ride in the bucket of the ladder truck and called me from the apex. As usual, the chief negotiated the price down, but taking delivery was the hard part. Hauling a very large ladder truck from one coast to the middle of the United States is an expensive proposition.

Upon his return, the chief checked with several trucking companies to find that it was near impossible to get the truck delivered due to its size. A few years earlier, we had shipped a smaller truck we purchased from the East coast on the back of a flatbed trailer. Chief found a trucking company that put him in contact with the seller and the delivery was made. That delivery was around $750.

Instead of looking for a delivery company, Chief decided to try a different tactic. He asked the dealer to deliver the vehicle for next to nothing. The dealer thought about it a day or two and called the chief back and stated that he had two men that would drive the vehicle from San Diego to Republic, Missouri. They would stay in Republic overnight and then fly back to San Diego. This would happen for the nominal cost of $2,000. That was a bargain due to the fact that those ladder trucks cannot go more than 50-55 miles an hour at best and burn gas excessively. The trip was approximately 1,600 miles. Think about driving 50-55 miles per hour for 1,600 miles in a vehicle that was not designed for the highway or highway speeds. When the ladder truck arrived, the total cost of purchase and delivery ended up right at $47,500. Mr. eBay did a nice job in saving tax dollars, keeping the fire department in usable vehicles and our I.S.O. rating low. It is also worth mentioning, the two gentlemen that drove the vehicle from San Diego, arrived on a Friday. That particular Friday night, Republic High School had a home football game. The two gentlemen had never seen a football game before. We take a high school football game for granted. Our visitors were excited to see one and our fire department members took the gentlemen to the football game, so they could enjoy their first game.

Another philosophy for elected officials is to stay out of the day-to-day operations. Some elected officials in communities with professional administrators or managers have an issue with involvement in day-to-day operations. Dean Thompson once told me that the mayor could be as involved or as uninvolved as they want at city hall. That is an accurate statement. As mayor of the city, there is never a lack of opinions being requested from city staff employees. It was my philosophy to let the city administrator manage the daily operations without my involvement. Some elected officials believe they have the right as an elected official to involve themselves in the daily operations. Once I became mayor, we added a council code of conduct that clearly stated that all council members were not to be involved in the daily operations and all staff contact flow through the city administrator and mayor. This was needed because we did not need a council member telling the public works director that a pot hole needs to be fixed on a certain street. The charter spelled out staff and elected official interaction. We wanted a council policy that was a little more specific in its outline of conduct. Elected officials need to know their role, understand their role and follow their role. This requires leadership that establishes the roles and holds members accountable for their actions.

Tornados

Growing up in tornado alley in Kansas, my family was used to seeing tornados and hearing tornado sirens. We can't forget the tornado drills in school where everyone went to the hallway and practiced the tornado position. Think of an airplane "crash position" while sitting on a cold tile floor in the school hallway pushed up against a painted cinder block wall or set of steel lockers. My upbringing was in Coffeyville, Kansas. The high school was named after a World War I fighter ace, Field Kindley. The mascot of the high school was appropriately named. We were the Golden Tornados. FKHS Golden Tornados. Tornados in that area of the country are common place and a person may get used to the drill after a while, but there is always a sense of uneasiness when the sirens sound. In Republic, tornados were common as well, but not as common as in Coffeyville. Republic had a series of tornadoes over the years. Two in particular stand out as exceptional. The first one hit Republic and taught me a valuable lesson in city government. The other was a massive tornado that hit a neighboring community.

The tornado sirens went off in the city on May 8, 2009 just as the tornado seemed to touch down on the west side of the community. The winds were strong at 110 mph, an EF1 tornado. The strong winds caused some damage to houses, uprooted trees and caused damage to other buildings along its path. One house was destroyed along the way. No one was injured. The damage was severe enough in one part of the community that the roads were blocked to ensure emergency workers could get to the area. The tornado touched down, stayed on the ground for a while and then went back into the clouds. Damage could have been worse if the tornado would have been on the ground longer. I had been mayor a little over a year. I was called to the fire station for a briefing from the emergency management director, city administrator, public works director, the police chief and the fire chief. We went over the area of destruction, our current response with the teams, next steps and plans for ensuring all were safe. The emergency management director told me the preliminary reports on the funnel cloud, the time on the ground, wind speed, direction and all other aspects of the tornado. He gave me the reports on the individuals in the destroyed home and the reports from all the houses that had been damaged. No injuries or casualties to people, but structures were damaged. The police chief gave me the report on exactly how the roads were being handled indicating limited access to the areas. The public works director gave me the information on the utility companies that were on the scene and that our public works employees and fire department employees were assisting them with turning off any utilities in the damaged houses. The fire chief gave me the information on any potential fire issues that could occur and an overview of fire coverage for the remainder of the city, since many of the fire department personnel were working in the affected area. The city administrator gave me a recap of the overall situation and requested information on what we needed to say to the press. All of these individuals had a great sense of humor. It was at this very moment that I realized that these are very professional people and dedicated to seeing the best for the community. The seriousness of the situation could be seen on their faces and the need for action could be sensed in their words. My leadership at that very moment was being tested. How would I react to the situation? Would it be with a nervousness or indecisiveness or calmness? My reaction would be mimicked by them. If I was nervous, they might be nervous, if I was indecisive, they would not be able to count on me for the tough decisions. If I was calm, they would more likely remain calm.

Calm ruled the day. They all gave me the rundown on the situation. I asked a few questions for clarification. At the end of the briefing, the fire chief looked at me and asked, "Okay boss, what would you like us to do?" They already knew what to do; they were looking for either my direction or reaffirmation of their decisions. My demeanor was calm. I stated that what they were doing was exactly what was needed. We briefly talked about communication between all of them and the community, especially the school district. The plan was created and followed from that point forward. A few weeks after this incident, we got together as a leadership team and discussed ways the situation could have been handled better. The consensus was that each department fully communicated with the other to effectively handle the situation and our biggest opportunity was to create a better line of communication with community organizations immediately after the crisis. An interesting learning occurred to me after the situation was over. In all of this communication during the crisis, the press was never around, nor were the council members, nor were any citizens. It was just the leadership team of the critical response areas of the city and the mayor was the leader of that group of individuals. The mayor had to be strong, calm and decisive in all situations. It also led me to the notion that being mayor was the ultimate back stage pass. I was there for the good situations and the bad situations, such as a tornado hitting the community.

The second tornado that was memorable hit Joplin, Missouri, on May 22, 2011. It was an EF5. It destroyed a major portion of the town. It was a deadly tornado with a 158 fatalities. Joplin was devastated and the storm was not done. Republic is slightly northeast of Joplin about 55 miles. This storm was initially headed to the northeast. It changed directions after leaving Joplin and went east with a slight southeast angle. It appeared that the supercell was headed toward the Republic area. From our previous tornado in 2009, all the leadership team members were communicating about our potential danger. This was discussed and we were prepared to take action if necessary. The state of Missouri sent communication that Joplin needed all the emergency assistance they could get. Our fire chief wanted to send our trucks down there immediately. At this point, the storm had not made it our way. Jim, the city administrator, told the chief to wait until the storm passed us without incident before leaving. It would have been detrimental to have an incident inside our community and our emergency personnel in transit to the Joplin emergency. We waited for the storm but we didn't wait long. It was on us, but it did not contain tornadoes. That part of the storm had actually gone further south towards the Branson area, but was west of Branson when more tornadoes touched the ground. None of them were as strong as the Joplin tornado, but tornadoes nonetheless. The clouds rolled over Republic and what we noticed were the things falling out of the sky; shingles, insulation, large pieces of tin, wood fragments and other things were raining as the clouds went over. This debris had been carried by the storm the 55 miles to Republic. As the storm reduced in strength, the debris fell out of the sky.

After the storm has passed and all was well with the city, the chief took our fire trucks and headed to Joplin. Missouri issued an aid request for Joplin through the Missouri State Wide Mutual Aid System. This request went to all municipalities in the state of Missouri. Mutual aid was also being requested and sent from Kansas, Oklahoma and Arkansas due to the proximity of Joplin to those states. Many other departments sent their trucks, vehicles and personnel and I-44 west was filled with emergency responders. The only issue was getting to Joplin. Joplin sat on the western border of Missouri at the Kansas and Oklahoma state lines with the Arkansas line about 52 miles to the south. I-44 was the fastest way to get to Joplin from the east. The debris that dropped on Republic was also being deposited on I-44. Roofing nails were everywhere and caused some issues with emergency vehicles as flat tires were rampant. The debris and flat tires only set back the volunteer effort for a while and the Republic fire department and police department joined with the other state wide volunteers to help in the rescue effort. Many lessons were learned on our end regarding preparedness as well as prioritization. A tornado like that could hit anywhere including Republic. It was our job to plan for the worst and hope for the best. The communication lessons learned in the 2009 tornado were put to use in the Joplin tornado. We communicated as a leadership team and were prepared in case the tornado had hit Republic. Some people are not rear-view mirror people. They don't look back to see what could be changed or how it could have affected them. They only look forward. In city government and emergency management, that is a poor policy. Being prepared is having the ability to answer the questions before they are asked and having a solution before the problem is in view.

Shut Up! Shut Up! (and Listen)

Expectations from the Top

ersonnel issues are guaranteed with any business that employees more than one person. City government is no exception and with 127 full time employees, we had our fair share of issues. One in particular sticks out in my mind. The finance director, Pete, had an issue with Jim the city administrator. The disagreement covered a lot of ground including Jim's wife working for him in finance, to the issues with the public works director to overall leadership of the city.

Pete was hired as finance director prior to me being on council in 2005. Pete took the city in a different direction than the previous finance director and took the department to a new level. He made as many changes as possible that the auditor recommended and worked on streamlining the city books. Pete did many positive things at the city and his knowledge helped move the city forward. Pete had a positive impact on the department. Over time his disagreement with Jim started to affect his ability to operate the finances of the city without prejudice toward others. In other words, at times, Pete let his personal views interfere with his professional views of the situation.

Each summer, Jim would take a vacation to Germany with a group of friends from his hometown of Chicago. This vacation would last about 10-12 days with Ron the city attorney filling in as city administrator while Jim was out of town. The disagreement between Pete and Jim seemed to be getting worse when Jim left on his vacation. While Jim was away, Pete decided to write me an email that outlined everything that was wrong with the city and Jim's leadership. He copied Ron and made several accusations that could not be ignored. Jim Huntsinger was also copied, since he was the Mayor Pro Tem at the time. Instead of emailing Pete with my response, I got with Ron and Jim Huntsinger to discuss next steps. The accusations were strong enough that we needed to meet with Pete. It was bad enough that Jim was absent and could not defend himself, but the timing of the email was planned to avoid Jim seeing it. I set a time in the afternoon on a Friday to meet with Pete. Pete, Jim Huntsinger, Ron and I were in the meeting. We went through the email paragraph by paragraph with Pete. Basically, he just did not like Jim as a person and did not respect him as a leader. It was clearly a personality conflict. Pete addressed the issues in an email and that did not fly with me or Jim H. or Ron. Pete sat across from me at the table, Jim H. was on my right at the end of the table and Ron was on my left at the other end of the table. At one point toward the end of the conversation, Pete put one hand on the table at the far right and put the other hand on the table to the far left with a large gap in between. Pete took his right hand and said that he was there, then took his left hand and said that Jim was there with the large gap in between. It was at this very moment that I reached across the table and put my hand in the middle of his hands in the gap and said, "My expectation is that you both are here." I stated that it is my expectation that he meet in the middle and that if he couldn't meet in the expectation, then he needed to decide what he wanted to do next. I told him that Jim would be receiving the same message upon his return from vacation and that his expectation would be exactly the same. I reiterated to Pete my expectation for him and pointedly asked him if he could fulfill my expectation. Pete did not know what to say. He was in a corner. The expectation was his to either meet or not to meet. The next move was up to Pete and he knew the consequences of not meeting the expectation. Jim H. told Pete that he may have been a retired colonel, but the commander-in-chief had spoken and he had a decision to make. Jim H. and Pete were both retired military and Jim H. put his comments in a framework that Pete would easily understand.

When Jim returned from vacation he was briefed on the situation by me and Ron. Jim thought personnel should have been involved with that serious of a breach of employee code. Remember, we had a strict set of guidelines for interaction with an elected official. It was my recommendation, along with Ron and Jim H that the decision on whether to meet the expectation lay with Pete. Personnel at this point did not need to be involved, they needed to be briefed, but not involved. This was due to Pete's direct communication and accusations to the mayor. The expectations were set by the highest elected official in the city with the support of the mayor pro tem and the attorney. Jim received the same conversation about meeting in the middle and the expectations moving forward. Jim said he would work with Pete. The next day Pete submitted his two week notice to resign. Pete said he could not meet the expectations set by the mayor and he knew the result would either be his dismissal or resignation. Pete took the resignation route.

Personality conflicts are prevalent in all businesses at some point and managing them through to a positive conclusion can be difficult. In our situation, I had to set the expectations moving forward and hold the individuals accountable for not hitting the expectations. Pete chose to not meet the expectation of working with Jim. It was his choice as it would have been Jim's choice as well.

In other twist of personality conflicts, the next finance director also had a personality conflict with Jim. It may seem that Jim was the common denominator in both of these issues, however the public works director also had a personality conflict Pete and the new finance director as well. It might be worth mentioning that the public works director also had a conflict with Jim and me. In the city government, the department leaders were the experts in their field and it was very difficult to get each of them to see the other's viewpoint. The underlying theme is that all of them dealt with personnel, which meant regardless of their expertise they had to be part time personnel directors inside and outside of their departments. This proved to be more difficult for some than others. The majority of disagreements involve a lack of communication or a lack of understanding of the opposing viewpoint.

The new finance director also had an issue with Jim, albeit for a different reason. Jim's wife Wanda worked for Laura, the new finance director. Wanda was promoted to Utility Billing Supervisor by Laura during Laura's tenure. It was this promotion that caused some issues in the department. Wanda had been at the city a long time and had a vast knowledge of every utility meter in the city along with many of the residents that used them. Wanda would do things her way and sometimes that was not what Laura wanted out of the Utility Billing Supervisor. Things began to get to a point where Laura wanted to give Wanda a written warning for her actions. Laura was not comfortable giving Wanda the warning since her husband was the city administrator.

Due to the situation with Jim and Wanda, we set up a different reporting structure for Wanda and Laura. We initially tried having Laura report to Ron, the city attorney, who would report to me on matters concerning Wanda. This went on for a little over a year, until we decided that this was not the best situation due to the city attorney acting as a department leader. In a case where his expertise was needed and it involved Laura or Wanda, he would have recuse himself and outside counsel would need to be hired. This did not work. We finally saw the light to make a change. We then moved Laura to report directly to me when it came to Wanda. Wanda reported to Laura, Laura reported to me. Jim was out of the loop when it came to any type of disciplinary action with Wanda.

Laura approached me with the situation and my comment was to follow the guidelines in the personnel manual. She needed to first try and correct the behavior, since that had not been addressed with Wanda. Wanda was doing what she thought was right and Laura had not fully explained the expectations moving forward. She assumed that Wanda would know when she clearly didn't know. My direction to Laura was clear. Lay out the expectations that Wanda is to meet and give her examples of the correct behavior along with the correct actions that need to happen. If Wanda didn't meet those expectations, the next steps would be to approach it from a personnel issue perspective with human resources involved. I gave Laura a deadline to outline her expectations to Wanda. Laura got busy on other things and did not hit the deadline. I met with her and outlined what needed to happen and when, but she was still reluctant to say anything to Wanda for fear of a reprisal from Jim. I gave Laura some time to think about our discussion on expectations and the fact that Jim actually reported to me and the council, therefore she had the backing of the elected body and the mayor. When she got back to me several weeks later, she said that she would just live with the issues instead of approaching Wanda. My comment was that she did not meet my expectations. It was rather disappointing to me that she would not take a professional approach to this situation, but I can understand her reluctance. I told her since that was her decision, that I did not want to hear any more complaining about the process Wanda was using. I do not remember the process in question, but I do remember that Laura wanted it done one way and Wanda was doing it a different way. Both processes seemed to work, but Laura wanted it done her way and I wanted Laura to be able to run her department without fear of retribution from the city administrator. It was left to Laura to make the decision on which process she wanted Wanda to use and it was clear that Laura didn't want the fight of enforcing her process. In hindsight, we should have never allowed the wife of the city administrator to work so close to him and I should have held Laura to the expectation and forced the issue. As they say, though, hindsight is 20/20. I liked Laura and Wanda and it pained me that we could not find common ground on this issue. There are times when people will not get along regardless of the circumstances.

Overcoming Turnover
in the Same Department

One of the areas of our municipality that seemed to have constant conversation over the years involved the planning department. At that time, the department consisted of a principle planner, senior planner, economic development director, building inspector and code compliance officer. As with any business, there seems to be departments that run smoothly with very little turnover and then there are departments where turnover is the norm. For several years, the planning department seemed to the department with internal issues along with higher turnover. This could be attributed to a variety of factors, such as, dealing with builders or developers that had an issue with an inspection or the process in which their permits were being reviewed. The code compliance officer also had their job to do and that usually entailed some sort of violation and/or fine. The building inspector had to follow the code and correct any issue at the building sites around the community. The planners had to ensure all plans matched the codes and zoning for the respective development. There were times that these plans needed changes to be up to code and that usually left the developer or builder spending more money to make the changes necessary. In all of these instances, the planning department had a tough job to do on a daily basis by the sheer nature of their interaction with the public and the policing nature of their roles.

During my tenure on council and as mayor, I can remember at least six planners working for the city. This turnover was not due to any one factor. One left to pursue a business opportunity in another state unrelated to municipal work. Another left to pursue an insurance position which is outside the planning field. Another left to become a planner at a smaller government, while another left to become a planner for Greene County. Another left to take a similar position at a municipality in Arkansas. In a bit of irony, the planner that left for Arkansas went to work in Siloam Springs, Arkansas for the city administrator there, David Cameron. After we hired David Cameron as the city administrator, he subsequently hired this planner and she moved back to Republic as the principle planner until she left a couple of years later.

The one planner that stayed through my tenure was Garrett Tyson. Garrett started as an intern with the city. He was quickly promoted to the planning department as the principle planner. Garrett had aspirations of becoming a city administrator. He would need all the experience a municipality could offer. Garrett worked hard and became an excellent planner over the years. He had a nice cool demeanor to him and was very calm when presenting information. One area that Garrett needed guidance was the application of code along with the ebb and flow of a negotiation. Garrett completed his jobs with a close adherence to the codes. This stance would, at times, get him sideways with builders, developers, engineers and others that had a vested interest in a project. The term "by the book" was often used in describing Garrett by builders and developers, although it was not always accurate. There are times to be strictly by the book and other times to review the entirety of the project before rendering a decision.

This close adherence to the code became important when it was applied to potential economic development. Garrett's supervisor was a person that did not have the background in the planning process. She did have a long history of negotiation and knew the ebb and flow of the negotiating process. The mixture of Garrett's planning knowledge and his supervisor's knowledge of negotiation would often clash when it came to what a development would be allowed to do on the property. On one particular project, a piece of property needed a road built, according to our codes and land use plan. The only issue surrounded the fact that there was a piece of property not owned by the developer that was between the proposed development and road that needed accessed. The public works department leader was involved and he was reluctant to build any road that he had to pay for out of his budget. He wanted the developer to fund it, while the developer wanted the city to build it. Roads are expensive to build, especially if it is a new build. Garrett proposed a myriad of proposals along with the developer, but the public works director did not approve of any of them. Garrett's supervisor worked hard to figure out a negotiation point where the road could be built and the development occur. It became a fight between the supervisor and the public works director with Garrett and the developer caught in the middle.

Garrett would create a proposal at his supervisor's direction, then send the proposal to the developer for review. The developer would send their comments back, then it would have to be reviewed internally with the public works director. Each time, there seemed to be another set of issues with the plans. This went on through the last six months of Jim Krischke's tenure with Jim getting involved attempting to reconcile the internal issue. Jim left for his new position and Jared Keeling, the interim city administrator was now at the forefront of the internal issue. In all fairness to Garrett, he did the best he could under the circumstances. This issue lasted several months until they asked me to become involved.

Garrett's supervisor left the city and we were in the process of hiring a new city administrator with the project still in limbo. Jared Keeling asked me to join the discussion. We worked through some of the internal issues without resolve on the project, when we hired David Cameron. David, Jared and Garrett worked on the project with the developer and had a resolution within six months of David's hiring. The internal issues with the public works director and the planning department were solved, for the most part, at this juncture.

This project taught Garrett a valuable lesson in code application and flexibility on developer projects. The knowledge that Garrett had on this project would serve him as he was promoted to the community development director position at the city. David changed the name from economic development director to community development director.

Side Story: Garrett would always get to the council meetings early, sit in the front row and review anything that he was going to present that evening. I would always make a point to arrive 45 minutes before the start of the meeting. This was done to accommodate anyone that wanted to discuss something before the meeting start time. Most of the time there were a few people that wanted to discuss something. If Garrett was there early, we would always have some type of conversation on a variety of topics before my conversations with the council members. Fast forward to my going away party as mayor – Garrett and I were having a conversation about his time at the city and how much I appreciated all the contributions he had made since he started at the city. It was at this time he told me a story that had me chuckle and remember that I had to watch what was said. He said one of his fondest memories of our conversations occurred before one council meeting. He told me that I had asked him if he had a tailor. When he said no, he then told me that I told him to go to the one I was using at the time and to get his pants properly tailored. He laughed about it, but actually took it seriously. I did not know he actually took my advice and from that point on, his pants were properly tailored. It was another off the cuff comment by me and taken seriously by the staff. As a leader, watch what is done and what is said.

Some Lessons are Verbal Some Lessons are Written

We had an issue with one of our police officers talking to local businesses about the internal mechanism of the city government. This in itself is not inherently bad, but when the officer is complaining about all of his perceived injustices and his idea to fix the issues, then it becomes a situation. One particular business was used by the officer as his favorite venting establishment. It also happened to be a local body shop where the owner was not happy with the city's rules on zoning requirements for his building. Information got back to the city administrator about the conversations that were taking place at this establishment between an on duty officer and the business owner. Some of the things that were being said were not accurate. The officer was supposedly speaking from a position of knowledge of the zoning and building codes.

The Police department did an internal investigation and found several other things that were going on regarding the officer and his lack of control over his conversations. All of it pointing at the negativity that was being spread by the officer throughout the community. The department also interviewed many business owners and found the same situation. A meeting was called with the human resource director, the police chief, the city attorney, the city administrator and me, since my name was actually brought up quite often in his conversations. Due to a phone call, I arrived late and they were laying out all the facts. The officer denied everything until the police chief presented the evidence and then the situation changed. The officer changed his attitude toward the meeting and apologized for the things that were said. The damage had already been done. I did not say anything up until the point where the police chief gave him the written warning. The officer did not believe his infractions were bad enough to warrant a written warning. He thought it should be a verbal warning without anything going in his file. It was at this point I spoke. My comments were brief and stated that some lessons are verbal and other lessons are written. This happened to be a written lesson for the very fact that the officer did not come clean with his comments immediately when presented the information. The human resources director followed up with the discipline policy and the leeway that it afforded the city on disciplinary matters. The officer knew that the written discipline was correct and did not fight it from there. It is worth mentioning that this officer was a few years from retiring and after this incident, the officer became a positive voice for the city in the community. In certain disciplinary discussions, as a leader, it is good to be to the point and decisive in your comments.

Restraint of Power is the Ultimate Exercise of Power

R estraint of power is the ultimate exercise of power. I wrote down that phrase in March of 2015 while thinking about the actual role of government officials in the situations that were encountered. The phrase was put to good use quickly. The city's budget was published and it showed the city with a large cash reserve. Jim Viebrock once stated that he always liked to read the paper to see how he was misquoted. (Jim termed out as a Missouri state representative, served as the Greene County presiding commissioner and was a Republic native.) In the case of our budget, it was actually misquoted. We did have a larger reserve than previous years, but the majority of the reserve was set aside for long term debt and accounted for in the budget. In other words, our finances looked good, but we didn't have as much of the excess cash as the paper made it seem. One of our public works employees decided that we as the leadership were not being forthright in our finances and that the city employees deserved a raise using this excess cash during the tough economic times. It is worth mentioning that we did not lay off or furlough any employees during the tough economic time of 2008-2016. This employee decided to write a letter to me outlining his thoughts on the matter. His thoughts included some not so printable accusations and character assassinations. Republic's charter clearly states how the interaction of employees and elected officials are supposed to be handled. Clearly his letter was way out of bounds with the charter. This type of letter would have probably gotten him fired anywhere else and probably should have from Republic as well, however we did not let our emotions get the best of us. The city administrator and I diagnosed the issue together coming to a few conclusions without the emotion that the letter certainly generated. The employee read the incorrectly printed budget numbers, did not fully understand that the numbers were incorrect, did not ask about the numbers, did not ask his supervisor about the numbers and fired off an email to the mayor. There were many issues within this situation and a few reactions that could have been taken. Several questions that consistently lingered, would the employee have written the letter if the newspaper would have published the correct information? The answer was probably not. If he had followed the protocol and discussed it with his supervisor first, would the employee have written the letter? The answer is probably not. If he had followed the correct protocol for contacting a public employee, would the letter have been received by the mayor? The answer is probably not.

We handled the issue with addressing the paper first to have corrected numbers printed. We then addressed the supervisor of the employee bringing him into the situation outlining the proper procedure along with his action plan moving forward with these types of issues. Just because the supervisor was not copied on the email and not part of the original issue, the supervisor is part of the issue and part of the solution. The supervisor needs to have control in the department and ensure all the employees understand the protocols that are in place for contacting a public official. Clearly, the employee either did not know or did not care about the protocols. This is where the supervisor would be involved. If the employee did not know, then it is on the supervisor for not educating the employees on the proper protocol. If the employee did know but did not care, then it is on the supervisor to take the proper disciplinary action. The supervisor fully understood his role in the situation and what would occur if something like that was repeated. The employee received the last discussion. We outlined what had happened, what should have happened and what will happen if something like that transpired again. The content of the letter coupled with the tone and accusatory nature of the letter could have been grounds for disciplinary action. After a full explanation, the employee agreed his response was not the right response nor did he follow the proper process to express such an opinion. In the business world, it would be similar to a first level employee telling the CEO what to do and where to go in a letter over something that was in the newspaper. There is a time and place for everything and sending a nasty letter to the mayor was certainly not the place or the time to do it. The employee kept his job and fully understood what would happen if something like that was repeated. Terminating the employee could have been completed based on how our charter was created on employee-elected official interaction. In this case the supervisor and the employee learned a valuable lesson and the employee kept his position. Restraint of power is the ultimate exercise of power.

Tragedy

Every community incurs accidents that cause communities to change laws. Many communities have the experience of losing students to car accidents or have other types of accidents that are never really forgotten. Republic was not any different and experienced a few accidents in a ten year span that killed students. Any life taken at an early age is tragic; however, any life taken is especially tragic.

One accident I will never forget. It did not involve high school students or anyone that I knew, but it left an impression that will last a lifetime. As mayor, there are things that will always be remembered, some good, some not so good. In this particular case, it is a not so good memory. While working out of my home office in March, 2013, my phone rang. It was Jim, the city administrator. Jim told me that an accident had occurred on highway 60 in front the Republic Ford Auto Dealership, on a very flat stretch of road. There is a stop light at that intersection and the speed limit was 40 mph at the time in both directions of the four lane road. The speed limit before that area was 60 mph coming from the east going west. It was a drastic change to go from 60 to 40 mph, but it was set up that way on that stretch of road.

Jim and I agreed to meet at the accident site. When I arrived, I saw a tractor trailer sitting in the middle of the intersection without anything in front of it. That would have been the logical place for an accident where a tractor trailer had hit someone or someone hit the tractor trailer in the intersection, but that was not the case. There were fire trucks and police cars blocking what was behind the tractor trailer. Sitting about 20 feet behind the tractor trailer that was in the intersection was another tractor trailer. Jim and I approached one of the fire trucks in the second lane shielding the accident area. One of the fire fighters stopped us and told us that we needed to be prepared for what we were about to witness. It was at this very moment that we noticed two of our own firefighters sitting on the bumper of one of the fire trucks with their heads in their hands. We briefly talked with them and asked them if they were okay. We received a few short answers and left them alone.

Upon walking around the fire trucks, we observed the first tractor trailer that was in the intersection and then another tractor trailer almost right behind it. What we were not prepared for was hidden in between the two tractor trailers. Directly in front of the second tractor trailer was a crushed new Chevrolet Silverado. The bed of the pickup had been crushed by the impact of the tractor trailer and the front of the truck was also crushed. In front of the Chevrolet Silverado pick-up was a Nissan Altima. The front of the Silverado was crushed from hitting the back of the Nissan. The Nissan was crushed underneath the back of the trailer of the first tractor trailer. Completely crushed, the back seat area was no more. The trunk was no more. The front seat was no more. All had become one with the driver in the middle of it. Both drivers were still in the vehicles and were declared deceased upon arrival of the emergency crews. Neither could be extracted due to the ongoing investigation and the fact that metal cutters would need to be used. It was a gruesome sight for anyone to behold.

The first tractor trailer was stopped at the light with the Nissan behind it and the Chevrolet truck behind it. The accident occurred when the driver of the second tractor trailer did not see the stop light or the 40 mph sign and plowed into the back of the Silverado, which in turn, plowed into the Nissan, which in turn plowed into the back of the first tractor trailer. The impact was so forceful that the first tractor trailer was pushed into the middle of the intersection. The driver of the first tractor trailer said his brakes were on and that he had no idea what was causing him to move. He was pushed half way into the intersection before his truck stopped moving. I do not remember if the first tractor trailer was full or empty, but even if it was empty, it would weigh close to 35,000 pounds. The impact was enormous.

The highway patrol was on the scene and had their investigation underway. The driver of the second tractor trailer was sitting on the ground by the highway patrol car. He was of Chinese decent and worked for a company out of Arkansas, even though he was from California. According to the investigation, he had been driving 70 hours over a seven day period violating the hours of service regulation. He falsified the driver's log book to cover the infractions. The highway patrol also checked the on-board computer and stated that the computer showed that he did not apply the brakes before the accident. His speed at the time was estimated at 50-59 mph. His name was Lei Sun and he eventually pled guilty to involuntary manslaughter charges and convicted to a four year prison sentence.

With any accident where death is involved, there are victims. The victims of this tragic accident were Corey Gresham and Lawrence "Mike" Coan. Mr. Gresham drove the Nissan and was from Macon, Missouri, visiting Republic on business. Mr. Gresham sold funeral supplies to funeral homes and was in Republic to visit one of his clients. Mr. Gresham was married with four children and one grandchild. Mr. Coan was retired and from Kimberling City, Missouri, about 45 minutes south of Republic. Mr. Coan was married, had three children and six grandchildren. Mr. Coan had purchased his new Silverado from a Chevrolet dealership in Republic and was returning to have the vehicle serviced for the first time. Many of us see, read or hear about accidents not paying too much attention unless we know the individuals involved. In every fatal accident, there are victims with a name, a face and a family.

The speed limit and the signage to this area were all evaluated with slight changes being made a few years later. The daughter of Mr. Coan wrote our city and praised our responders for their efforts at the scene. She was a first responder herself and understood the toll that it takes to be at accidents like that one. She was very gracious in her loss, something we could all apply during times of loss.

Betty Called, We Listened

In every community there seems to be an individual or set of individuals that like to keep an eye on the city government. In Republic, that person was Betty North. Betty would attend almost every council meeting, planning and zoning meetings along with many other civic events. It seemed that Betty was everywhere and when she had something on her mind, she would not hesitate to call the person that she needed to discuss a topic. After my first election on council as a representative for Ward 3, the mayor and the city administrator stated that Betty would likely be calling me over issues that pertained to the city. Most of the issues that Betty addressed revolved around planning, zoning, platting and the process associated with each. She was interested in ensuring that we correctly followed the process in regards to community communication. She would ensure that we followed the proper procedure for advertising for each rezone and ensure that the proper documentation was on the proposed property. In my view, this was actually quite helpful, but most of the planning department staff did not view it as helpful. They would complain to the city administrator and to the mayor, even though Mayor Collins would be receiving his own phone calls from Betty.

Betty did not have an issue picking up the phone to call the mayor or the planning department or any other person associated with the city. Her goal was to ensure that the city did things the right way in the right time using the right process. The mayor and the city administrator did not seem to want to engage Betty very often and it seemed that they felt they had engaged her too much for the time it took for them to answer the requests she made. My first phone call with Betty lasted a good couple of hours. The second phone call and many subsequent phone calls lasted over an hour. There were short phone calls with Betty and many long phone calls. In the end Betty did make many excellent points. There were some items that we agreed upon and many items that we had to agree to disagree. It was never personal with Betty when she called. She was looking out for the community and an understanding of the government process without being inside the government.

Until my first election as mayor, the staff seemed to view Betty as a time consumer for them and did not completely engage Betty. After my first election as mayor, I told Jim and the city staff that our interaction with Betty North would change. We would listen to Betty and take her call as we did all of the citizens in Republic. She was to be treated no differently and we should answer her questions honestly, even if that answer was unknown and we would have to call her back. Engage Betty and listen to her thoughts.

Betty would continually attend council meetings and let us know her thoughts on issues. The majority of time, Betty was fully prepared with a hand written statement that she had timed to ensure she stayed under our three minute limit on public comments to the council. The three minute limit was a carryover from Mayor Collins time and continued during my tenure. We would allow the speaker to go longer if we were told upfront that the comments may take longer than the allotted three minutes. There were a few times when Betty knew her comments would be exceeding the three minutes. In each instance, Betty was always upfront with us on the time and asked our permission to exceed the three minute limit. She was always approved to exceed the limit and was always cognizant of the council's time.

During my fourth term as mayor, we had a public hearing on a proposed public zoning classification change. The public hearing document was read by the staff and then I opened the meeting for any comments by the public. At all public hearings, I opened the public comments by stating, "Anyone wishing to speak **_for_** this particular item, please come forward, state your name, sign in and give us your best three minutes". Once all those people were finished, then I would state, "Anyone wishing to speak **_against_** this particular item please come forward, state your name, sign in and give us your best three minutes." Once everyone had their comments heard, we would close the public hearing. At this particular public hearing, I chose to switch the "For" and "Against". In other words, the people speaking against the public hearing item went first and the people speaking for the public hearing item would speak last. This is the complete opposite on the direction that is given to the audience on public hearing items.

This particular public hearing did not have anyone speak for or against the item and the public hearing was closed, but that was not the end of it. The next evening after the council meeting, my phone rang. It was Betty North. She accurately corrected me on switching the "For" and "Against" and I agreed with her to keep it in the correct order from that point forward. It may have been a small break from the proper cadence of the public hearing process, but Betty caught it and wanted me to ensure that proper process was followed. I very much appreciated the detail in which Betty observed the City government mechanisms.

There were times when Betty would seek information through a freedom of information request. Many inside governments view any request through the freedom of information act as a way to use the information against the government. They would create roadblocks to the information access. These road blocks could consist of cost or time or any other item that could be considered detrimental to the access of information. In our case, Betty did watch us very closely and would apply the information back to us if something was uncovered that did not follow the process. As with all requests, hers was researched and a cost to retrieve the information was given. This was a standard operating procedure and Betty was not treated any differently than anyone else. Betty would pay the price for the information and it was given in a timely manner. Regardless of whether we thought it would be used against the city or whether it was just for her knowledge, the information request was processed and handled like any other citizen or government agency requesting information.

Betty took a keen interest in our planning and zoning board and would attend almost as many of those meetings as she would attend city council meetings. One of the mayor's duties is to appoint members to the P&Z board from each of the four wards. We had an opening on the P&Z board in Ward 1, Betty's ward. I approached her about serving on the board; after all, she watched it very closely and was very well versed in the process. To my surprise, Betty declined my offer. Betty had many things going on around the community including her rental houses and being a master gardener. She did not feel that she wanted to invest that much time in P&Z. I pointed out that she was already spending the time by attending meetings and doing research. She agreed but turned down the offer. A few nights later, Betty called me and asked if I had filled the open P&Z position. Since it had not been filled, Betty asked me if her husband George would be a possible candidate for the position. After talking to George, I presented him to the Council at the next meeting for appointment. He received a unanimous vote and was appointed to the board. This appointment would allow Betty to know the inner workings of the P&Z board without actually being involved.

We strove to make the governance of the city more efficient and effective every year. Over the years, Betty could see that we were getting better and better with each passing year and her attendance at council meetings slowed substantially. Before my last election as mayor in April 2016, Betty called me and heard that I was running for mayor a fifth time. Betty told me that if I had a campaign sign that she would put one in her yard. That was the ultimate stamp of approval for me regarding Betty North. We engaged her from day one, listened to her, treated her fairly and made necessary changes. She had become a believer in the process of government change in Republic. Betty North may be just one person in a community of 17,000, however change occurs on a one-on-one basis and Betty actively involved herself in the government process in Republic to assist in that change.

Appointments, Lots of Them

The mayor was charged with appointing individuals to a variety of boards and commissions within the community. Appointments did not occur on a consistent basis with some only occurring once during my tenure. Below are the main areas of appointments:

City Council: All wards during non-election cycles when an opening was available.

Planning & Zoning: One representative from each ward when an opening was available.

Capital Improvements Committee: When an opening was available.

Housing Commission: When an opening was available.

Municipal Judge: For new terms and when an opening was available.

Reserve Judges: For new terms and when an opening was available.

City attorney

City clerk

In the eight years as mayor, appointments were made in all areas listed with several on the city council and planning & zoning. The appointment process was fairly straightforward. An opening would have to be available and it was up to me to find a qualified individual to fill the position. P&Z was a two year term with reappointment at the end of the term, if the person wanted to continue. Capital Improvements was basically a limitless appointment. The individual could remain on this committee as long as they met the requirements for committee. Housing commission had terms similar to P&Z without election.

The city council operated differently compared to the other appointments. An appointment was made only when an opening was available and that appointment was only applicable until the next election. For example, a council member in Ward 3 resigns from the council in July and was just elected two months before in April to a two year term. I would appoint a person to fill that council seat until the next election in April. The actual term remaining for that position was over a year and a half on a two year term. The appointee would have to run at the next election ten months later in order to remain in the position. Likewise, if the council member leaving only had six months left on their two year term, the appointee would have six months on the council before the next election. This was created to ensure that a person could not fix the election system where one person could win the election, resign the next day and the mayor appoints someone for their entire term. An appointed council member had a limited number of months to be on council before an election.

During my eight years as mayor, I appointed council members in every ward except Ward 2. Gerry Poole and Garry Wilson were constantly elected in ward 2 every year, so we never had to appoint in that ward. Yes, their names are spelled correctly. Ward 3 seemed to be the most transitioned ward. I can remember at least five appointees in that ward alone.

The municipal judge position in Republic was held by Judge Andrew Hager for my first ten years on council. When Judge Hager retired, we conducted interviews of various candidates. The interviews were conducted by a committee led by the city attorney and city administrator. Once they finalized their list, they gave me the recommendation and I interviewed the candidate. The candidate was Ryan Ricketts. I interviewed Ryan and outlined my expectations for our municipal governance. Ryan fully understood the vision of Republic and his role as municipal judge in the process. He was presented to the council on February 14, 2014, as the municipal judge appointee and the council unanimously voted in favor to appoint him.

Likewise, the reserve judges were interviewed by the committee and they presented their recommendations to me. This time, no additional interviews were needed and the reserve judges were voted on and approved at the same time as Judge Ricketts. There were two reserve judges that were available in the case where the presiding judge could not hold court for whatever reason.

All appointments had to be presented to the city council and voted on for approval. If the appointee was not approved, then it was up to me to present another individual to fill the position. In eleven years serving on the council, there was not one appointee that was rejected. It is worth mentioning that our city council was not elected as Democrats or Republicans. Political parties were not part of our voting or elective process. Betty North asked me one time which of our council members was Democrat or Republican. It was a question that I had never really thought about, since we were not elected as part of a political affiliation. I honestly answered her that I did not have a clue and it did not matter to me. She agreed and was actually glad we did not have political affiliations as part of our governance. Our role was to represent the citizens and help move the city forward.

Chain the Doors
Call the Press

n Republic, the school district was a separate taxing entity without any managerial connection to the city or county. The district operated separately financially and was governed by a school board along with their leadership. The city and the school seemed to work together when necessary but there were several times over the years in which the district and the city were at odds with each other. In 2009, the school district was building a new high school. As a taxing entity, they were held to a standard that, at times, did not require city approval on some of the building processes. This is not an issue in most situations, but it became an issue quickly toward the end of the project. The district wanted to move into the building in January of 2010, so the first graduating class would be 2010. This would have been fine except the building was not fully completed and there were a few issues that our inspectors wanted fixed before the city issued an occupancy permit.

The superintendent of the district basically stated that we did not have the authority to deny them occupancy based on not having an occupancy letter and stated they would occupy the building when they wanted. This did not set well with our inspection staff due to many concerns. We tried all communication lines we could to work with the district on completing the most dangerous issues, as we saw them, before they sent 1,200 plus students into the building. Our communication and pleading was ignored by the

159

district and they set a date. A couple of construction delays moved the start date until the second week in January and they were still pressing forward.

At the city, a meeting was held to discuss next steps and the issues involved. What we heard from the fire chief was rather disturbing. There were several areas in the building in which the firewall was not installed with a few of the areas critical for any type of fire suppression. Without the firewall installed, a simple fire in one area of the building could have quickly spread throughout the entire building with little hindrance. Many other items were brought forth, yet none of the items compared to the fire suppression issue. It was time to discuss the issues directly with the superintendent and the president of the school board. Jim Krischke set up the meeting with the two school personnel and me, just the four of us. It was a cold early January afternoon and snow had started. The weather was a premonition for our meeting it seemed.

We met in the planning department board room and right from the start it appeared the superintendent had no intention of fixing or completing any of the items on our inspection list. During our conversation, the superintendent attempted to close his notebook several times which was his indication that in his mind the meeting was over. In each case, I told him we are not done and he reopened his notebook. After about an hour of not getting anywhere with our discussion on the life/safety issues, the superintendent closed his book and told us there was really nothing that the city could do to stop them from opening the school. He basically went on to tell us that they would take all our suggestions from the inspection and review them as part of their construction review after the entire project was completed. This was unacceptable to me. He was blatantly putting the students' lives at stake without a care because he promised a school board or the community that he would be in that new school by a certain date. An artificial deadline took precedence over the safety of the students.

With his last comment about our inability to do anything, I relayed to him our actions for his push to occupy the building. I told him and the president of the school board that we would have our police department and fire department put chains on the doors and arrest anyone that tried to enter the building. We would also call the media to have them on hand, so we could tell them exactly why we were chaining the doors. The superintendent was correct that the district really didn't have to fix many of the inspection items, due to their status as a taxing entity. When it came to life/safety issues, the city had the final say on occupancy. The superintendent told me that would not be good press for the city. He was right, on that point. I told him it may not be good press for us, but it would be devastating to the school district and something that the parents would question for years to come in any instance where a student was injured on the school grounds. Our meeting ended with the two of them knowing exactly what we were prepared to do in case of any attempt to occupy the new building.

The next day our fire chief received a call from the school districts construction company wanting to go over exactly what was needed on the firewalls and the location for their construction. The firewalls were constructed and the school district worked on many of the items on the inspection list. We did not give them an occupancy permit until we were satisfied that all the major infractions were corrected. The district still did not complete our entire inspection list, but committed to correct the issues at a later date. All the life safety issues were corrected and the students were allowed to occupy the building.

This was not typical of our partnership with the school district and it would take a change of leadership in order for it to change.

School District Change
and the S.A.C.

The communication lines between the city and school district had become strained since the new high school occupancy incident. We still worked together on a variety of projects but complete lines of communication were not fully engaged. Several incidents over the years, including a book banning, within the school district caused them to not renew the contract of the superintendent. The search for a new superintendent started in early 2012.

In July, 2012, Chance Wistrom became the new superintendent for the school district in Republic. Mr. Wistrom had been hired from a smaller school district about 20 minutes away from Republic. Immediately upon his arrival, communication improved. Through mutual communication, a lunch was scheduled with Chance, Jim and me. We discussed a variety of topics with improved communication at the forefront of the conversation. It was clear that communication between the two entities was essential. School construction projects required city assistance, city road/street issues required the school to be informed for bus routes, snow routes and emergency procedures. Many other activities all required a working cooperation from each entity.

We discussed a few ways to create those types of communication lines. During our brainstorming session, it occurred to me that we were already doing something at the city that could work with the school district. I told Chance about our PAR group and how effective it allowed us to be on a litany of projects. I suggested that we create a group like the PAR group, meet every month and have an agenda that would keep us updated on items between us. We all thought that was a great idea and came up with the first date for the meeting. While we were discussing some of the first agenda topics, I threw out an acronym that we could call the group. S.A.C. It stood for School and City. I even tossed in a tag line, "Tackling community issues together". Both the acronym and tagline stuck.

An agenda and a list of attendees were agreed upon. From the School, it would be the school board president, the superintendent, the public relations officer, one of the assistant superintendents and the school resource officer director. From the city, it would be the mayor, city administrator, mayor pro tem, planning/economic development director, city administrator administrative assistant, public works director and the police chief. Occasionally, we would have visitors join the group when a topic involved them in the process of communication.

The S.A.C. group started an avalanche of information between the two entities. Many items were created and formed from the S.A.C. group.

Resource officer vehicles. The school district had three resource officers tasked with covering five grade schools, a middle school and a high school. This was not an easy task and the officers had to use their own vehicles. Funding vehicles on a yearly basis could be very costly. We proposed a plan that would help the district put their resource officers in district vehicles at a minimal cost.

Several years before, we implemented a vehicle replacement matrix for our police department that would replace three vehicles every year. The three used patrol cars were then sent to auction and three new ones were purchased. This occurred every year and eliminated many pitfalls of attempting to replace the majority of the vehicles all at once. The cost could be budgeted each year and would allow newer vehicles to be on the road. It helped the budget and the image of the department.

Our idea was to give to the school district the three vehicles getting retired for a period of one year. They would drive them for a year and then return them to us so we could send them to auction. We would then give them the three vehicles being retired that year for their use. Eventually, as our vehicles were replaced with newer models, the school district would be driving the same type of vehicle as our officers. The only cost to the district would be the sign on the side of the car and possibly the light bar on top, in case we needed to reuse it. They would have Republic Resource Officer on theirs, while we would have Republic Police on ours. The color of the cars would be identical. This program was vetted at the S.A.C. group and approved. This started in 2014 and continued through my time at the city.

The school bus partnership. The Republic parks department had an older school bus that was used in the summer program to shuttle kids to the programs and activities. The bus was older and only got used during the summer. We were discussing the school bus at one of our S.A.C. meetings due to the fact that we needed some maintenance and repairs on the bus and were looking to the school district for advice on the company that conducted their repairs. It was at this time, one of the school officials suggested we create a program similar to our police car/resource officer vehicle program. The program was created and vetted at the next S.A.C. meeting with the school district allowing us to use one of their busses during the summer to shuttle the kids. This worked out well for us since our old bus had a propensity to breakdown at the most inopportune times in the summer.

Cooperation and communication were keys to the success of both entities. The S.A.C. group also established guidelines for communication on a variety of topics. Snow removal on the streets was overlaid with bus routes to ensure we hit the bus routes while removing snow. School incident response process was coordinated where training took place at the same time with both entities. Emergency communication was reviewed and updated. Each entity had a contact priority list and we ensured both entities had an updated list at all times. This was put into application during the tornados and other emergency situations where it worked extremely well.

Communication can solve many issues. Two-way communication is required to be fully successful. The school and the city agreed that communication from both entities was required for both to be successful.

Leadership is not for those
that want to be in charge

It has been said that government should run more like business. This can be true in certain aspects of government, but not all. There is a reason for the process and like most business process, something occurred to change or modify or add a process. That is why there are strange laws on the books all over the country. Something happened that required action by a municipal government or state government. Government and business are not so far apart in how they operate. Any large company requires a certain process for things to be accomplished. In those businesses, many of the decisions can be handled within the realm of a few individuals or departments. Government is really no different. The size of the organization in business or government dictates the processes that are in place in order for it to operate. The larger the entity, the more processes are in place to operate.

Leadership, in government or business, contains a multitude of applications and learnings. There is not one business book that applies universally solving all the problems for the leader. Most leadership books outline several premises and back it up by examples that reiterate why it worked from them and why it will work for you. There are some excellent books that can be applied in many situations. The idea is to take all the learnings possible and apply what is appropriate for that situation. There are times when we need to be compassionate and there are business book examples for that to be applied. There are times when we need to be firm and there are business book examples for that to be applied. From my time at the city, leadership encompassed a realm of learnings and applications from a variety of sources. Take this book, pick out what you can apply in different situations and use it.

Leadership should not be for those that want to be in charge. Leadership is for those that want to make a difference and have the ability and skill set to move an organization forward, business or government.

Short Stories from the Front Line of a Municipality

The following are several stories from my time in office. Some are humorous, some serious, some have leadership principles while others are just occurrences. If there is one thing to be said about government, it does encounter all aspects of life.

Satellite radio can lead to poor timing. Keith Roberts, one of our council members, had invited Mayor Collins, Dean Thompson the city administrator and the assistant city administrator Chris to lunch one day. Keith was listening to a comedy channel on satellite radio on the way to city hall to pick up the three. The radio was rather loud, according to Keith. He shut off the vehicle and went inside to get the gentlemen. As a reminder, Mayor Collins was a Baptist pastor. They all get in the truck with Mayor Collins sitting in the front seat. Keith started the truck and then the satellite radio came on at the same high volume that it was when Keith turned off the truck. The only issue was at that very moment a comedian was in the middle of a profanity laced joke. Keith could not find the volume button fast enough – he did not know whether to hit the volume button on the steering wheel or reach for the knob on the stereo. Once he finally got the radio turned down, Mayor Collins broke the ice and stated that, "We have all heard those words before."

You're the next mayor. In February 2008, I had a surgery on my throat which encompassed having stiches in my mouth. One evening while watching television upstairs, I felt something drop in my mouth. My mouth quickly became warm. I ran to the bathroom and spit up blood. Lots of it. One of the stiches had fallen out and the bleeding started. The sink was filling up fast. I yelled to my wife downstairs to call 911. I didn't know if I was going to pass out from losing so much blood or what was going to happen. She asked me who she was supposed to call. When I shouted 911 again, she then had a small panic in her voice and complied. It was a cold February evening with about two feet of snow on the ground. The roads were snow packed and covered. It would have been almost impossible for Diane to put me in the car to drive to the hospital. When the 911 call went over the scanner, the Fire Chief, Duane Compton, heard it and drove to our house immediately. He lived in the next subdivision and was close to us. The Republic fire department responded as well. When Chief Compton arrived, he hit his brakes to stop in front of the house, but slid about thirty feet too far. He came in the house and found me on the floor in the front room downstairs. Diane had helped me get there from upstairs and I was laying down hoping that would help stop the bleeding. The fire truck arrived along with a couple of Republic police officers. I was basically the interim mayor, since I was running unopposed with the election in April and Mayor Collins concentrating on his state campaign. I appreciated the quick response. The fire department personnel helped me off the floor and examined my throat. The bleeding had stopped, but we didn't know if it would start again. A trip to the emergency room was required. I asked Diane to call my doctor to let him know the situation. She could not find her glasses, so she asked Chief Compton to help her find the number. Chief could not find his glasses either since he rushed out of the house so quickly. It is worth noting that Diane and Chief Compton grew up together in Republic and were good friends. Chief Compton helped me in to the kitchen. He wanted to wipe off some blood from my face before my ride with EMS. EMS had arrived several minutes after the fire department. They were waiting for me to finish in the kitchen to transport me to the emergency room. While at the kitchen sink washing the blood from my face and hands, Chief Compton grabbed a paper towel. He handed it to me and said, "Here, wipe the blood off your face, you're the next mayor."

Watch what you *say*, it could lead to change. As the mayor, people in general listen to what you have to say. In a community the size of Republic, the mayoral position carries some weight since Republic's municipal government is one with a strong mayor position and a city administrator. There is a difference between a city administrator and a city manager. In our case, the mayor was a strong position. Before a council meeting one night, Jim Krischke, the city administrator, and I were discussing several things. Since we sat side by side, it was difficult to look at each other. We would talk at each other's ear since many of the things we discussed were not for public knowledge. While he was talking to me before the meeting, I was listening to him and looking up at the ceiling in the council chambers. There were three rows of lights with about five light fixtures in each row and drop ceiling tiles in between. The lights in one fixture had one color of fluorescent bulbs, while another fixture had another color fluorescent bulb. There were at least three different colored fluorescent lights illuminating the council chambers. I inquired about a few things and we were done with our conversation. After we concluded our conversation, I made a passing comment that one of these days we might want to replace the lighting in the council chambers to have all one color of fluorescent bulbs. It would look more professional and create a nice environment in which to work. Two weeks later at our next council meeting, all the bulbs had been changed to the same color. Progress sometimes occurs when the leader makes a comment. Note to self: as a leader, watch what is said, no matter how trivial, someone will take it seriously even if it was an observation or just a comment. Thank goodness.

Following the Sunshine. The Greene County Mayors Association elected me President of that organization and re-elected me a few more times during my tenure as mayor of Republic. The association encompassed all the mayors in Greene County, including Springfield the largest city in the county. The media attended the Mayors Association quite often due to the agenda usually addressing something that was an overall county issue. The leadership of Greene County along with the Greene County sheriff would also attend. At one particular meeting, we were discussing the correct process to work through an agenda item at one of the communities since that mayor wanted to ensure they were following the correct process. During this discussion, one of the mayors from a smaller community made the comment that he "didn't follow the Sunshine Law and that it was a bunch of bunk". The press seemed to be writing or recording every word. As my father once told me, "Never argue with a person that buys their ink by the barrel or argue with someone who has the microphone." In either case, you will not come out on the right end. Lucky for that mayor, another topic took precedence. It became heated with the leadership from Greene County. His quote about the Sunshine Law never made the paper or the news.

<u>Where is the Headstone?</u> A few public works employees were out working on a stretch of road in town. While walking through the ditch in the tall grass, a worker came across a headstone for a grave at a cemetery. It was not engraved but was extremely heavy. The workers carefully loaded the headstone into a city vehicle and took it back to the public works department. The city clerk called the local funeral home and inquired without any result. The local curators of the cemeteries could not provide any information regarding the blank headstone either. The city clerk decided to put a note about the headstone in all 6,000+ water bills that went to the citizens. After a few days, the city clerk received a response. A gentleman named Ron came to her office and described the headstone perfectly and stated that it was his. Ron relayed the story about transporting it and when they arrived at their destination the headstone was missing from the vehicle. They looked about everywhere, but did not find it. Ron was reunited with the headstone. The employees of the public works department loaded it into his truck for another ride, this time secured in the bed of the truck. Interestingly enough, at the time Ron was a council member in ward 1.

<u>Orange whip, orange whip</u>. After becoming mayor, Jim Krischke the city administrator and I had a very similar sense of humor. Movie quotes were often integrated into conversations much to the dismay of the staff and council. Jim was the city administrator from 2007-2016, from Chicago and the Blues Brothers was one of his favorite movies, since it was based in Chicago. At one point in the movie, John Candy (as a

police officer) asked his fellow officers if they wanted an orange whip. He pointed at each one of them and asked, "Orange whip? Orange whip?" getting an orange whip total for the waitress. This movie line would sometimes get quoted by Jim or me when we were out to lunch together. It would also play a part in a council meeting.

The council celebrated birthdays every time we had one for a council member or city leadership team member. One year, Jim decided to serve orange whips for my birthday during the council meeting. At the beginning of the council meeting, Jim had the council sing Happy Birthday. He proceeded to give all the council members and me orange whips. The only issue with the celebratory drinks is that they were in a tall, plastic margarita style stemware with a little umbrella on top. One of the council members was a Baptist pastor, the one that Mayor Collins appointed years earlier. He served his appointment and then was elected a couple of more times in Ward 3. He didn't want to be seen on the local cable channel with a plastic margarita style drink with an umbrella in front of him, so, he politely moved the drink to the floor beside him. I can understand why he did it, but it always had me wondering would people really think that we were drinking alcohol at a council meeting that was televised with a Baptist pastor as a council member and sitting right next to him was another council member that was a wife of a retired Baptist pastor? Probably not, but the council member that was the wife of the retired Baptist pastor finished her entire orange whip with the umbrella mounted on top on public television for all to see.

<u>Taking care of one of their own</u>. A man was driving home in his car one night and had apparently been drinking, heavily. He was traveling at a high rate of

speed and lost control of his vehicle. The vehicle crossed into a ditch, jumped the two opposite direction lanes and landed on a few vehicles at a local business. That business just happened to be a local bar. The driver exited the vehicle, but could not apparently stand up or least stand upright for any length of time. When emergency personnel arrived, the driver was sitting in a chair next to the accident with his vehicle on top of the other vehicles. The patrons at the bar had brought a chair outside for the man to sit in until the authorities arrived. He was uninjured.

<u>South Manure Road</u>. Highway 174 was a two-lane east/west road that connected the city of Mt. Vernon 15 miles to the west and the city of Republic. Highway 174 ran through the north side of Republic and had a mixture of use along its trek. There were businesses at the beginning where it connected to Highway 60 in Republic. Schools, a park and then houses went through Republic finally ending with a horse ranch at the edge of town. A city sewage truck was traveling east down Highway 174 after it had finished picking up a "load" from one of our pump stations. Sorry for the pun, but it was true. Apparently, one of the service technicians had left a valve open on the sewage truck. It was dropping sewage along the way as it traveled with the drivers unaware of their deposit on the road. Once they figured out they were leaving a trail of gross along the highway, they pulled over the side of the road to correct the issue. The only problem at this point, there had been many cars driving along that same road at the same time. Now, one would think that people would see that it was raw sewage and either avoid it or take a different route. That was not the case. Cars were not avoiding it, just driving through it as if it were some dark brown snow. It is hard to believe that people would not pay attention to that type of road condition.

People do tend to not pay attention to a lot of things going on around them. In this particular case, it was a messy and foul-smelling lesson in lack of attention.

Movie references are fun for the insiders. At one particular PAR meeting, we were discussing an economic development project where the adjacent property would be used as a road to the project property. Jim Krischke was at one end of the table and I was at the other with all the other attendees on either side of us along the table. There was a lot of discussion regarding this project due to the number of obstacles and hurdles that would need to be overcome to make it work. The adjacent property was the same size as the project property but had highway frontage along one side. The project property did not have direct access to the highway and needed it due to the type of business and the number of trucks that would be involved. The adjacent property was not part of the project and was targeted in the city's master transportation plan as having a road going through the middle of it to serve the project property and property further in the development. The adjacent property had one issue for a road to be through the middle of it. It had a pond in the area where the road was planned. The public works director was sitting to my right and Jim's left when he made a comment about the pond. He stated, "It is a nice piece of property, but has a pond in the back." This caused me to say, "It has a pool and a pond." To which Jim replied, "The pond would be good for you." Those are quotes from the movie Caddyshack and no one else caught the reference except for Jim and me. Connie said she did not have shorthand for movie quotes, so they did not make the minutes.

Paneling is so versatile. As mentioned in a previous story, Republic city hall was a conglomeration of three buildings. All were older with a variety of different wall coverings, carpet and decoration. Over the years, the city updated the areas to which the public was exposed. The back hallway into the break room was not one of those areas. It still had the wood paneling that it was shod with many years before. The carpet had been replaced, but the paneling stayed around for some reason. I would always joke with Jim, the city administrator that the paneling was next on the list to be updated. He would take the opposite stance that he really liked the paneling since it was so versatile and that it took him back to his childhood home where paneling was everywhere. He said it allowed him to be relaxed when walking through that area. This went on for a few months until one day I was at city hall and decided to take an informal survey on whether the paneling needed to go or stay. Jim thought this would be a scientific way to decide on whether to update or not to update. Out of the 12 people that voted in the building, the vote went 11-1 to discard the paneling for something else or just paint over it. Jim was the lone vote to retain the paneling. Shockingly, when the budget came up for the next year, there was not any funding appropriated for paneling repainting or repair or removal. Jim "manipulated" the budget to keep funding from the update. This "manipulation" went on until 2016. Jim had resigned and took a city administration position in Maryland Heights, Missouri, a suburb of St. Louis. The interim city administrator was Jared Keeling. The first day without Jim, I asked Mr. Keeling if his maintenance staff would have some time for a project, not telling him about the project. Mr. Keeling inquired and they were actually fairly busy with other projects and would not be available for a month or two. Mr. Keeling became curious, since I did not make requests of the staff or inquire about availability very often. When I told him of the paneling update project, Mr. Keeling said it would be added to the list along with the other projects that were already on the schedule. I left thinking that it would not be completed for a while since the projects in front of it were much more pressing and needed. A week later I went to city hall to sign a batch of business licenses and noticed the hallway was much brighter. The paneling project was complete – fresh paint over the paneling, new tile floor in the break room and a new back splash above the counter. Jim was correct; paneling is indeed versatile – especially when it comes to paint color. It can be painted almost any color and still look like painted paneling, albeit much better looking than brown paneling.

Time flies, literally. During a PAR meeting, the budget was the topic of conversation and how we could continue to keep a full staff without laying off people during the tough economic time. My mayoral time coincided with the economic stress of 2008 all the way through 2016. We would figure out a way to cut costs or other measures to remain solvent with all the employees intact. Many municipalities were laying off people or eliminating positions to get their budgets under control. We never had to eliminate positions or lay off any people during that time due to the budget. While at this particular PAR meeting, the finance director at the time, Pete, made a comment that if we would force annex a local business then our budget would be whole with their tax revenue. The business was inside our urban service boundary and right on the border of our city limit. An annexation would have been an easy solution, but it would have been a forced one since the business did not want to be inside our city limits voluntarily. Pete continued the conversation of force annexation and made a comment that since our economic development director had not been able to secure a volunteer annexation that we would need to force the annex. This conversation was not the first time that Pete had used this line of thinking to solve the budget issues. Pete was retired Army and had worked for the federal highway department in Arkansas and retired there as well before working for the city of Republic. It is worth mentioning that Pete was also good friends with Mr. Huntsinger. The PAR meeting had been going for almost an hour and Pete would not leave the forced annexation conversation. At one point, Pete said something derogatory to the economic development director and that was all I could take. No more Mr. Nice guy. I stopped Pete in his comments and told him it was my turn to weigh in on this subject. In no uncertain terms, Pete was told to drop the forced annexation of this business and to never bring it up again. Yes, a couple of profane words were thrown in for good measure, not my style but they slip every now and then when I get really upset. Not sure how Connie was able to write those in shorthand, but they should have made the minutes. About the time I was almost finished, Pete started to talk again and interrupt me, which did not set well with me. The public works director got up to leave for either more coffee or to the bathroom or for cover, but as he walked out, I got really upset and slammed the door to the conference room right behind him so my directive would only be heard by the individuals in the room. The nice clock on the wall behind me came crashing down under my feet, which really got me upset, so it was kicked to the side of the room and hit the base board. A few more terse words from me mixed with a profane word and the conversation was complete. I said "next item" and that is the last time that we ever had the conversation over forced annexation of that business. In leadership, it is good to show a little emotion every now and then to ensure that people know where the decisions reside. In this case, Pete knew he was not the highest ranked individual at the table. The meeting was very productive and went very quickly after that point. The clock still worked and was there when I left - after it was put back together. It is amazing how time flies.

Do your homework. Before my first council meeting as a council member, a brown envelope was delivered to my house. It contained the documents for the meeting. It was interesting due to the fact that it was delivered by a police officer. The city clerk at the time did not prepare the packets in time for pick up on the Thursday or Friday before the meeting. They would be completed and delivered via the police department. After Brenda was hired as the city clerk, the police delivery ceased. The packets were always ready the Thursday before the meeting for all council members to pick up at the city clerk's office. At one memorable council meeting, Ms. Poole, one of the longest standing members of council and former Mayor, asked that an item be tabled. When asked why she wanted it tabled, she calmly stated that she didn't have time to read her packet before the council meeting. The item was not tabled and the vote continued. During my first full meeting as mayor, we had an executive session and my direction was to read their information packets before the meeting and do the homework necessary to make an informed decision on all items. We had removed all the barriers from the packets not being ready to the police department delivering them late. There were no excuses now to not be prepared. Ms. Poole got the message and was always well prepared in our meetings. At least she was honest about stating that she did not read her packet, all of it on cable tv and recorded.

Fire truck photo bomb. The fire chief had worked a cooperative agreement with several other departments for a multidepartment purchase of fire trucks. The specs for each truck at each fire department may have been slightly different, however the idea of purchasing in bulk made sense. They shopped this idea to the fire truck manufacturers. They found one that agreed to the prospect, met the specs and proceeded to build all the vehicles. Many municipal vehicles can be purchased on a state bid. Police cars, sheriff cars, public works trucks, etc., can all be purchased on a state bid in Missouri. Fire trucks are the exception. By combining their purchasing power, the departments collectively received the truck they needed at a reduced cost. The city of Republic received their truck and the chief called me one day to ask me to attend a photo session in Springfield with the other fire departments and their trucks. The idea was to get all the trucks together and showcase how the program worked with the departments. I rode with the chief in the new fire truck. It was an interesting ride. Fire trucks are not fast, but they sure seem steady with all that weight. We arrived and the photo session took place. Each truck was photographed separately and then all were photographed as a group. The news media were in attendance to report on the story. It was held in a large empty parking lot with only the large parking lot lights on it. Each light had a large concrete base. After everything was completed, the chief, without me in the vehicle, backed up our truck to make room for another truck. We were standing near another truck while he moved our truck. Once it was moved, the chief came around from our truck with an angry look on his face and a few profane words in his sentences. I am sure those profane words were not correctly used, since he may not have been able to properly diagram them in a sentence. We inquired what had happened. When he backed up, he did not see the concrete base that grounded the very large parking lot light. Chief hit it! The nice new chrome bumper was no more. The picture in the paper showed the group of fire trucks. The damaged light post was in the background like a photo bomb. It was a good ride home, though. I rode with the city administrator in his car.

Watch what you **do**, it could lead to change. After my comments about the lights and Jim having all the lights in the council chambers changed to match, I had a tendency to watch what I said. It was before another council meeting that Jim and I were talking about a variety of topics again when I noticed the ceiling tiles were different colors and different textures. The drop ceiling tiles would get wet or get deformed over time and need to be replaced. Well, our maintenance crews were very efficient the majority of the time. They would change out the tile in the quickest time possible to go on to more important tasks. Could not blame them, ceiling tiles would not be high on my list if there were other tasks that needed to be accomplished, but the council chambers were the face of the elected body. The maintenance crews would change out the ceiling tiles with whatever ceiling tile they had at the time or whichever one fit. Color and texture were not high on the criteria list when replacing the tiles. It reminded me of the joke about picking out socks with the same texture and forgetting about the color. It worked, but didn't match. The ceiling tiles were in that kind of disarray. I must have been bored, because I counted no less than four different colored ceiling tiles with a variety of textures. All were in the white spectrum of color. Not one of them would qualify as bright white. So, instead of saying anything to Jim, I started tallying the number of different colors of white that were on the tiles and the number of different textures that were on the ceiling tiles. The meeting had not started, but Jim and I had finished our conversation. Jim noticed my tally notations and was curious about what I was doing. Ron, the attorney also noticed, but in typical Ron manner, he looked at me and said, "What on earth are you doing?" I explained to him the tally marks and what I was doing while waiting for the meeting to start. We started at 7:00 p.m. not a minute before and usually not a minute after. Ron looked at me, looked at Jim and then they both looked at the ceiling tiles. They both decided to see if my tallies were correct and started their own research. Luckily, it was time to start the meeting and neither finished their count. At the next meeting, all the ceiling tiles were the same. Same color, same texture and all installed properly.

Who pays for lunch? Toward the end of my last term as mayor, David Cameron the new city administrator wanted to have a luncheon to discuss a variety of topics with the staff executive management team. All the department leaders were in attendance, including Connie the executive administrative assistant and Brenda the city clerk. After the lunch portion, we discussed our topics and were ready to leave when David asked, "Who pays for lunch?" The department leaders all stated that luncheons like that were never approved. I asked Connie and she stated that "They never approve the luncheons on the expense report." All the department leaders agreed with Connie. Keep in mind every department leader is in attendance, the city administrator, assistant city administrator, the mayor and the finance director. Everyone in a leadership position in the city including the highest elected official is sitting at the table. So, my questioning continued to everyone, "Who is 'they'?" All of them looked around and I flatly stated, "Every leader for the city of Republic is sitting at this table. There is no 'they', it is us and David is approved to purchase everyone's lunch."

Sometimes, we get caught in how things have always been done and do not stop to think about how things could be done.